MILTON

A Topographical Guide

Sister M. Christopher Pecheux

UNIVERSITY
PRESS OF
AMERICA

LANHAM • NEW YORK • LONDON

Copyright © 1981 by

University Press of America,™ Inc.

4720 Boston Way
Lanham, MD 20706

3 Henrietta Street
London WC2E 8LU England

Library of Congress Cataloging In Publication Data

Pecheux, M. Christopher (Mary Christopher),
1916–
Milton, a topographical guide.

Bibliography: p.
Includes index.

1. Milton, John, 1608-1674--Homes and
Haunts. 2. Poets, English--Early modern,
1500-1700--Biography. 3. London (England)--
Biography. 4. London (England)--Description--
Guide books. I. Title.
PR3584.P4   821'.4   81-40626
ISBN 0-8191-1953-9   AACR2
ISBN 0-8191-1954-7 (pbk.)

MILTON: A TOPOGRAPHICAL GUIDE

CONTENTS

iv

LIST OF ILLUSTRATIONS

vi

PREFACE

The purpose of this _Guide_ is to present accurate
and up-to-date information on the places in England
that are of special interest in the context of Milton's
life and works. The format reflects this purpose. In
the first chapter there are entries, arranged chronologically, for the places in which he lived, including the
history of the area and relevant information on the parish churches connected with his residences. The village
of Chalfont St. Giles and the churches of St. Margaret
and St. Giles Cripplegate are placed in a separate chapter and treated on a different scale, since they have
extensive associations and have remained much as they
were in the seventeenth century. Other places of interest to Miltonists -- churches and other monuments --
are described in a third chapter. Finally, there is a
chapter on the events which have left a particular mark
on Milton's London.

Each entry is preceded by information on how to
reach the locality and followed by bibliographical references. The latter are in shortened form, giving only
author and page number (unless an author cited has more
than one work in the bibliography, in which case the
proper identification is made). Full information for
each item will be found in the bibliography. This
method of documentation has been adopted in view of the
fact that the book, though arranged chronologically, is
not primarily a biography. Interested specialists will
be able to find additional material by using the references given at the end of each section; in the few
cases where the facts in question are not generally
agreed on, a specific reference has been given.

With one exception, the dates of Milton's various
changes of residence (give or take a few months) are
not in dispute. The exception is the year of his re-
moval from Jewin Street to Bunhill Road. Following
Edward Phillips, who says that the move was made not
long after Milton's marriage to Elizabeth Minshull
(which took place in February 1663), biographers before
Parker suggested that year as the date. Parker, however, in his exhaustive 1968 biography, cites four
pieces of evidence (in addition to Phillips' demonstra-
ble inaccuracy in some other dates) to place the move
several years later, with 1669 or 1670 as a plausible
hypothesis. I have followed Parker's dating. (See
his _Milton_, 2 vols. [Oxford: Oxford University Press,
1968], II:1125-26.)

The orientation of this <u>Guide</u> precludes treatment of the period (1638-1639) which Milton spent traveling on the continent, an interval for which we do not have the relatively abundant data available for all the other periods of his life. Such information as exists has been well treated by John Arthos in <u>Milton and the Italian Cities</u> (New York: Barnes and Noble, 1968), and a brief summary of the known facts can be found in Hanford and Taaffe, <u>A Milton Handbook</u>, 5th ed. (New York: Appleton-Century-Crofts, 1970), Appendix F.

I wish to express my gratitude to the libraries of the places where I have worked, particularly of the Gill Library, College of New Rochelle, and of the New York Public Library, where I have used not only the main reference collection but also the resources of the Local History Division, the Prints Division, and the Map Division. A grant from the College of New Rochelle enabled me to visit the places in England described in the book. I am grateful to Karen McCann for the three maps and four drawings which she made and to Susan Korn for her photographic work on some of the other illustrations, as well as to Barbara Albanese and Mary Stoner for their typing skills.

The following have graciously given permission for the reproduction of illustrations for which they hold the copyright: the British Tourist Authority, New York City, for the photographs of Ludlow Castle, St. Margaret's Church, and Milton's cottage at Chalfont St. Giles, as well as for the map of modern London on which the three maps in the Appendix are based; Gordon Fraser Gallery Ltd. for the view of the interior of St. Giles Cripplegate; the Guildhall Library, City of London, for the sketch of St. Giles Cripplegate in the eighteenth century; the London Topographical Society for the diagram of Bread Street and for details from the Society's 1905 reproduction of Newcourt and Faithorne's 1658 map of London; the New York Public Library for Hollar's engraving of St. Paul's in flames, as well as for the Library's copy of the Newcourt-Faithorne map; the Rector of the Priory Church of St. Bartholomew the Great, London, for the photograph of the Elizabethan gatehouse at its entrance.

INTRODUCTION

Speaking of Milton, Samuel Johnson observed in his
<u>Lives of the Poets</u>: "I cannot but remark a kind of re-
spect, perhaps unconsciously, paid to this great man by
his biographers: every house in which he resided is
historically mentioned, as if it were an injury to
neglect naming any place that he honoured by his pres-
ence" (<u>The Six Chief Lives</u>, p. 72).

Johnson spoke truly, but where is the tourist or
even the average scholar who today could name or locate
those places? Anyone asked to name the greatest English writer after Shakespeare would unhesitatingly say,
"Milton"; and every tourist pays a visit to Stratford;
but Milton excites little curiosity. Few are even
aware that there are places which recall his memory.
If we have Shakespeare's birthplace, we have Milton's
cottage at Chalfont St. Giles; if we can stand beside
Shakespeare's grave in Holy Trinity Church in Stratford,
we can do the same for Milton at his grave in St. Giles
Cripplegate. Moreover, because Milton lived in London,
in several different areas, and because we know a great
deal more about his biography than we do about
Shakespeare's, there are many more places of interest
associated with him.

More than a hundred years ago an anonymous writer,
pleading for a memorial in the Church of St. Giles,
sketched some of the possibilities:

> In the case of Shakespeare, little is
> known of the man. We are but scantily
> informed of his habits and the details
> of his life, and our interest is prin-
> cipally excited by the consideration,
> that in him, England produced the greatest

1

dramatic author the world ever saw.
A commemoration of Milton would,
however, embrace more than a recognition
of his poetic fame. The man himself --
his principles of action, his conduct,
his whole life, -- all are before us,
and we can follow him step by step
from the cradle to the grave. (A Milton
Memorial, pp. 19-20)

To follow Milton from the cradle to the grave is
not, indeed, a new venture. The great nineteenth-
century biographer, David Masson, having gathered all
the relevant material in his six-volume Life of John
Milton (1859-1880), later collected the data on
Milton's residences in a series of articles in an ob-
scure periodical (Good Words) and published the same
material a year later (1894) as a chapter in a book he
edited, In the Footsteps of the Poets. In 1903 Lucia
Mead published a book on Milton's England. J. Milton
French, in his monumental collection of Life Records
of John Milton (5 vols., 1949-1958), included extensive
information on the residences and also published in
1949 an article on "Milton's Homes and Investments."
William Riley Parker has most of the same material
scattered through his Milton: A Biography (2 vols.,
1968). Parker augments or occasionally corrects some
of the information given by French. Although many un-
answered questions remain, little of importance has
been added to our knowledge of Milton's life since the
publication of these two works.

Without the labors of Masson, French, and Parker
the present project could not have been written. Yet
none of these earlier studies fulfills the need which
this one is designed to satisfy. The passage of time

2

and the changes resulting from the bombing in World
War II have made much of Masson's material, as well as
Mead's, obsolete. French's 1949 article is useful but
confines itself to bare facts concerning the residences,
not including topographical background or references to
places other than the homes, while the material in the
Life Records and in Parker's biography is also largely
compressed and widely scattered. Finally, Don Wolfe's
Milton and His England (1971), despite the title, is of
an entirely different nature: its scope includes the
history of Milton's times, and the textual matter is
subordinate to the illustrations.

    With the biographical information found in scat-
tered sources the present study has combined the results of extensive research on the history and topog-
raphy of London. The collocation of the material on
London, past and present, with what is known of Milton's
life and writing has not been done in just this way in
any existing work. Some of the information, such as
the background on the churches of St. Giles and St.
Margaret, may be new even to seasoned Milton scholars,
who may also be glad to refresh their knowledge of
more familiar places.

    In any case, I have a broader readership in mind.
In this age of specialization there are innumerable
well-informed and respectable scholars who know the
outline of Milton's life but have never made a point of
following him from the cradle to the grave. Many of
these visit England, and many would be interested in
coming into contact with places which have Miltonic
associations. Their students, too, are traveling in
increasing numbers, as are intelligent and well-read
tourists who are not students. For all these, visits
to the places here described will be interesting and

3

rewarding. To paraphrase Marjorie Nicolson's observation that to know the works of Milton is to have a liberal education, it can be said that to have followed Milton's footsteps is to have seen a great part of London. Casual tourists and seasoned scholars alike who, however great their interest, cannot carry with them French's five volumes or even Parker's substantial two may, it is hoped, find the present guide useful as they make their pilgrimage to these literary shrines.

CHAPTER I

FROM THE CRADLE TO THE GRAVE

1608-1632: BREAD STREET

(BREAD STREET is close to three Under-
ground stations. Walk east from St.
Paul's or west from Bank on the Central
Line or north from Mansion House on
Circle and District. Bus Nos. 8, 22,
25, and 501 go along Cheapside.)

The house in which Milton was born on Friday, 9
December 1608, stood in BREAD STREET, which runs south
from Cheapside, just west of Milk Street and east of
Wood Street. Today its southern limit is Cannon
Street; in 1608 it continued to Thames Street, below
which many small lanes ran down to the river (in the
third of a mile between the Bridge and Queenhithe there
were twenty-four lanes, alleys, and yards).

An important street from early times, it gave its
name to a ward; the "Warda de Bredstrate" is mentioned
in 1285. The proximity to the river, then a main highway for traffic, was an advantage to merchants who
lived there. Like the neighboring Milk and Wood
Streets, it derived its name from the product in which
it specialized. In 1302 Edward I had decreed that no
baker should sell bread from his own house or shop but
from the market in Bread Street. By the seventeenth
century Stow could describe it as "now wholly inhabited
by rich merchants; and divers fair inns be there, for
good receipt of carriers and other travellers to the
city." Still more prosperous was the part of Cheapside
near Wood Street known as Goldsmiths' Row, where ten
dwelling houses and fourteen shops, all in one frame,
were adorned with the goldsmiths' arms and figures cast
in lead, richly painted over and gilded, "the most

5

beautiful frame of fair houses and shops that be within the walls of London, or elsewhere in England." The street was probably important enough to be paved; throughout the century, in general, there were many courts and alleys which had no pavements at all, but the more important streets were paved with cobblestones or flat stones.

One of the establishments for travelers to which Stow refers was the Mermaid Tavern. Of the several taverns in London bearing that name, the oldest, the most important, and the one best known to literature was situated on the west side of Bread Street, near Old Fish Street (which has now been absorbed by Queen Victoria Street). It was famous for its fish dinners. Since its nearness to Blackfriars Theatre made it popular with dramatists and actors, it is not fanciful to think that Milton as a very small boy may have passed Shakespeare on the street. Later it was a rendezvous for Ben Jonson and other writers. The famous tavern was sometimes referred to as "Mermaid in Cheap," but Rogers has shown (in The Mermaid and Mitre Taverns) that it was actually in Bread Street, some distance south of Cheapside. Jonson's Epigram No. 133 celebrates its good cheer: "At Bread Street's Mermaid, having dined, and merry,/Proposed to go to Holborn in a wherry." It was possible then, and indeed much later, to travel to the northern part of the city by way of the Fleet River, which was not completely closed over until the second half of the eighteenth century.

About eight years before Milton's birth his father, a scrivener, had rented the house which was to be the poet's home for the first thirty-two years of his life. That it was owned by Eton College is a gratuitous gift of fortune to the Miltonists of the

6

world, for to this fact we owe the preservation of detailed plans and descriptions from a survey made in October 1617. The occasion was the granting of a lease to one Sir Baptist Hicks for a large building, known as the White Bear, on the corner of Cheapside and Bread Street. Parts of the building were sub-let to other tenants, of whom the principal one was Mr. Milton. His shop was known as the Spread Eagle, signs such as this being the principal means of identification before street numbers came into use in 1760.

The entrance to the Milton home, at the southern end of the property, would have been about seventy-five feet down from Cheapside on the east side of the street. The scrivener's shop occupied the ground floor. At the end of a passageway were stairs leading to the first floor, which had a wainscoted hall and parlor, a kitchen, buttery, and counting-house. On the next floor were a large wainscoted bedroom and two other rooms. Two other floors contained less elaborate rooms.

The house was left to Milton on his father's death, and although he was no longer living there it was still his when it was destroyed by the Great Fire in 1666. It is pleasant to know, however, that it was for at least a brief space a place of pilgrimage, for Aubrey tells us that the only inducement of many foreigners to visit England was to see the Protector Cromwell and Mr. John Milton, and they "would see the house and chamber wher he was borne." For many years the spot was marked by an inscription, but today there is nothing. The street, heavily bombed in World War II, was widened somewhat in the subsequent rebuilding and the area once occupied by the house is covered now partly by the street, partly by a supermarket. The visitor may walk mournfully up and down its aisles and hope that the

7

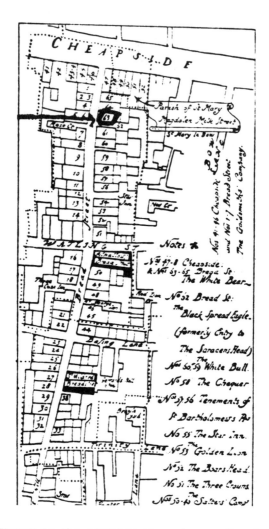

Bread Street in the seventeenth century. Based on the plan of John Ogilby. The arrow at the top (added) points to the location of Milton's birthplace. Reproduced by permission of the London Topographical Society.

City will soon place at least a plaque on the corner of the building; some steps towards this end have been initiated.

(Besant, 13; Blakiston, 2-3; Brett-James, 41; Darbishire, 7; Ekwall, 72; Fletcher, I:26; French, Life Records, I:14-19; Masson, Life, I:32; Parker, I:5-6; II: 698-99; Rogers, "Bread Street," 71; Rogers, The Mermaid and Mitre Taverns, 6-9, 27-35; Rogers, Old Cheapside, 10; Smith, 28; Stow, I:295-96, 344-46.)

The Parish Churches:

A short distance away, at the southeast corner of Bread and Watling Street, was the CHURCH OF ALL HALLOWS, where Milton was baptized on 20 December, 1608. Seven years later a younger brother, Christopher, was baptized here, preceded by two girls, Sara, who lived only about a month, and Tabitha, who survived about a year and a half.

At one time it was thought that the baptismal font had survived the destruction of the church during the Great Fire, but it seems that the font in question (the cover of which is now in the church of St. Andrew by the Wardrobe) came from the church which was rebuilt by Wren in 1680. When the church was demolished in 1877, in the process of widening Upper Thames Street, a tablet bearing a medallion of Milton was placed at the site. But the tablet in turn disappeared during the bombing in World War II and has not been replaced.

A memorial of the baptism does remain, however, in the nearby church of ST. MARY LE BOW on Cheapside just east of Bread Street. This ancient church, which dates at least from William the Conqueror, was the first church in London to be built on arches, whence it derived its name: St. Mary de Arcubus or Le-Bow. Of

the original Norman church the only remnant now is the
crypt. The Ecclesiastical Court of Arches sat in Bow
Church, and bishops attended here to have their elec-
tion confirmed. Its bells are well known because of
the saying that true cockneys are only those who are
born within their sound.

Although the Milton home was within the boundaries
of the parish of All Hallows, St. Mary le Bow was just
as close. It too lay in the path of the Great Fire and
was rebuilt by Wren, only to be destroyed again in 1940.
The Wren steeple, however, still survives.

When the Church of All Hallows was demolished, a
tablet which had been placed there early in the nineteenth century was brought to St. Mary le Bow, where
it may now be seen fixed on the outside of the west
wall. For the literary pilgrim it is the most concrete
memorial associated with the birthplace. Above the inscription may be read the lines which Dryden prefixed
to the fourth edition of Paradise Lost, published in
1688:

> Three Poets, in three distant Ages born,
> Greece, Italy, and England did adorn.
> The First in loftiness of thought Surpass'd;
> The Next in Majesty; in both the Last.
> The force of Nature cou'd not farther goe:
> To make a Third she joyned the former two.

The inscription itself reads:

> "John Milton, was Born in Bread Street on Friday.
> the 9th day of December. 1608. and was Baptised
> in the Parish-Church of All-Hallows Bread
> Street on Tuesday. the 20th day of December. 1608."

Some time after 1876 a stained-glass window showing the expulsion from Paradise had been placed in the

wall of St. Mary le Bow close to the tablet: this was
destroyed during the bombing and not replaced. The
baptismal register from All Hallows remains in the
church.

For American visitors St. Mary le Bow has a particular interest because of its connection with Trinity
Church in New York City. Trinity received most of its
land by grant from William III in 1697, and the King
named St. Mary le Bow as a model for the New York parish to follow. The first bell in Trinity was a gift
from the Bishop of London in 1704. In 1947 Trinity
sent a gift of $50,000 to be used in the reconstruc-
tion of the bombed London church.

(Allison, 324; Bulmer-Thomas, 4; French, I: 2-8;
Jenkinson, 179-82; Kent, Encyclopedia, 3rd ed., 105,
145, 183; Parker, II: 699; Smith, 14; "For Favore Received," Time 50-76; Venables, 454.)

St. Paul's School:

> (The site of ST. PAUL'S SCHOOL, is
> just east of the Cathedral; the
> nearest Underground station is St.
> Paul's, on the Central line. Bus
> Nos. 4, 8, 22, 25, 141 and 502 are
> the most convenient.)

At some time during his childhood (perhaps as
early as 1615, perhaps not until 1621, shortly after
his twelfth birthday) Milton became a pupil of ST.
PAUL'S SCHOOL. Founded by the great humanist John
Colet about 1510, the school was at the east end of
St. Paul's Churchyard, a very short distance from the
Milton home. We can still follow the route, turning
right on Watling Street and walking the brief block to
New Change. It consisted of a central building of one
story, with houses of several stories at each end. An
inscription on a wall on the west side of the street

11

today marks the approximate site of the school which
Milton attended. Rebuilt after the Fire, the school
was re-located in Hammersmith in 1884 and then moved
again to its present location in Barnes.

The enlightened humanism of the school owed much
to its founder, who continued to be venerated. When
Colet died in 1519, he was buried in the Cathedral, and
the Mercers' Company (the governing body of the school)
erected an elaborate monument, including a bust executed by Pietro Torrigiano (1472-1528), with prose in-
scriptions in Latin and English and elegiacs by
William Lilly. The Mercers' Company restored and em-
bellished the tomb in 1575-76 and again in 1617-18.
With the rest of the cathedral, the tomb was destroyed
in the Great Fire of 1666.

St. Paul's School as it appeared before the Fire of
1666. Drawing by Karen McCann from an engraving by
Thomas Holloway in Vol. VI of London, ed. Charles
Knight (London, 1851).

Early in the sixteenth century, however, a cast of
Torrigiano's bust of Colet had been made and was later
installed in the school hall, over the chair of the
headmaster, replacing the image of the Child Jesus
which had held this place of honor in the founder's day.
Strype, writing in 1720, relates the strange story of
the survival of this bust:

> At the upper end of the School,
> facing to the Door, was a decent Cathedra,
> or Chair placed, somewhat advanced, for
> the high Master to sit in, when he
> pleased, and to teach and dictate there.
> And over it was a lively Effigies, (and
> of exquisite Art) of the head of Dr. Colet,
> cut (as it seemed) either in Stone or
> Wood; and over the head in Capitals, Deo
> Opt. Max. Trino et Uni Joannes Coletus
> Dec Scti. Pauli Londin. Hanc Scholam
> Posuit. . . .
>
> But this Figure was destroyed with
> the School in the Great Fire; yet was
> afterwards found in the Rubbish by a
> curious Man, and Searcher into the City
> Antiquities, who observed (and so told
> me) that it was Cast and Hollow, by a
> curious Art now lost.

Once again, therefore, the bust was placed over
the Master's chair and continued to look down on generations of schoolboys. It was still there when
Donald Clark published his study John Milton at St.
Paul's School in 1947, but, though still owned by the
school, it is now on indefinite loan to the Victoria
and Albert Museum. Here, in Room 52, we may gaze at

the one surviving material link with the pre-Fire school. There is also a replica of the bust in the National Portrait Gallery.

(Clark, 34-40; DNB, 782; French, Life Records, I: 7-8; Hare, I: 129-35; Knight, IV: 265-66; V: 227; Parker, I: 13; Rossiter, 292.)

St. Paul's Cathedral:

Although Milton has no direct ties with the Cathedral itself, his attendance at St. Paul's School certainly made him familiar with it, and its tower dominated the landscape of his early years. The church stood on a site once occupied by Romans and Britons where the Saxon Ethelbert, King of Kent, erected a Christian church, which was rebuilt successively in medieval times. Its lofty spire was destroyed by fire in 1561, but even without it the tower rose 285 feet. The building needed repairs, however, and in 1620 its restoration was inaugurated with a royal procession. By 1643 everything except the steeple had been repaired.

On the very eve of the Great Fire plans were being made for further restoration, but the old cathedral was destroyed in the fire, and the cornerstone of the new one was not laid until a year after Milton's death.

While Milton was still living in Bread Street and attending St. Paul's School, John Donne was Dean of the Cathedral (1621-31) and John Tomkins was organist (1619-38). The latter was associated with John Milton the elder.

Up until the time of the Fire St. Paul's Churchyard was the principal center for booksellers,

14

undoubtedly visited by Milton from time to time. After
the Fire many of the booksellers re-settled in nearby
Paternoster Row or moved northward to Little Britain.

(Clark, 34-35; Hare, I: 129-15; Knight, IV: 265-66,
V: 227.)

Christ's College, Cambridge:

> (CAMBRIDGE is easily accessible by car;
> it is sixty-five miles north of London,
> on the A-10 trunk road or the M-11
> motorway. Trains run frequently from
> two main-line London stations, Euston
> and Liverpool Street, and the journey
> takes a little over an hour. The
> journey by bus, from the Victoria Coach
> Station, takes about two and a half
> hours. CHRIST'S COLLEGE is on the east
> side of the north end of St. Andrew
> Street, between Christ's Lane and the
> beginning of Hobson Street. Bridge
> Street and Sidney Street lie north
> of it.)

On 12 February 1625 Milton was admitted to
CHRIST'S COLLEGE in CAMBRIDGE UNIVERSITY, and matricu-
lated on 9 April. From then until 3 July 1632, when
he signed the graduation book for his A.M. degree --
that is, for more than seven years -- most of his time
would have been spent here.

Christ's College today has not greatly altered
since the seventeenth century. It is situated at the
northern end of St. Andrew's Street, which is a con-
tinuation, curving to the east, of Bridge Street and
Sidney Street. In 1625 the land to the immediate
north and east was open but cultivated.

We may still enter the great gateway and, going
through the archway past the porter's lodge, locate the
windows of the rooms which Milton occupied. These are

15

on the left side, just to the right of the first staircase on that side, on the "first" floor (i.e., first
according to general European usage, the floor which
is level with the ground being called the ground floor
and the one above that, the first; Americans would
speak of the ground floor as the first and say that
Milton's rooms were on the second). The apartment,
consisting of a small study with two windows looking
into the court and a very small bedroom, would have
been shared with others. Since it is still occupied,
it is not usually open to visitors. One can, however,
look up at the windows and perhaps recall another
literary memory: Wordsworth recorded in "The Prelude"
that his excitement at attending a party in the very
rooms once occupied by Milton moved him to a series of
toasts to his memory, so that for the first and only
time in his life he became drunk:

> Among the band of my compeers was one
> Whom chance had stationed in the very room
> Honoured by Milton's name. O temperate Bard!
> Be it confest that, for the first time, seated
> Within thy innocent lodge and oratory,
> One of a festive circle, I poured out
> Libations, to thy memory drank, till pride
> And gratitude grew dizzy in a brain
> Never excited by the fumes of wine
> Before that hour, or since.
>
> Wordsworth, "The Prelude," Book Third,
> (Residence at Cambridge, lines 293-302)

Farther on in the First Court is the door of the
Master's Lodge, with the original carving over the
doorway still intact; to the left, the chapel, substantially unchanged; and to the right the Hall, which
has been rebuilt but which retains some original

paneling in the Screens at the end. In the upper right hand corner there is now a bust of Milton, often copied, which is almost certainly an authentic likeness, probably made during Milton's lifetime.

In the Second Court, dominated by the Fellows' Building, erected in 1642, was a building known as Rats' Hall in which Milton may have had quarters during his first year at Cambridge. This was a small wooden structure built in 1613 to take care of a sudden rise in enrollment and apparently intended to be temporary. As a historian wryly remarks, "'Temporary' college buildings, however, are sometimes long a-razing," and the hall was not pulled down until 1731.

The Second Court leads into the Fellows' Garden, where near the far end may be seen the so-called "Milton's mulberry tree." Most authorities scorn the tradition that it was planted by Milton, but at least it may be true that he sometimes sat beneath its shade, since it was probably one of a number of trees planted in 1608. At the far end of the garden is a pool adorned by a row of busts, Milton's among them.

Among the other buildings at Cambridge which date from Milton's time and which he must have visited are the chapel of King's College, with its magnificent fan vaulting, and Great St. Mary's, the University Church, a short distance west of Christ's College.

(Christ's College Cambridge, 4; Fletcher, II: 13, 24-27; French, Life Records, I: 90, 93, 148; Masson, "Local Memories," 41; Parker, I: 24-25, II: 726, 949-50; Sloane, 357-58.)

1632-1635: HAMMERSMITH

HAMMERSMITH is only a few miles from
Central London, to the southwest.
Hammersmith Road is the westward con-
tinuation of Kensington High Street;
at its junction with Fulham Palace
Road stands the parish church of St.
Paul. Since other main roads also
converge on the spot, traffic is very
heavy. Piccadilly and District Underground lines have a station at Hammersmith; Bus Nos. 9, 11, and 73 are convenient from Central London.)

At some time during 1632, the year Milton left
Cambridge, the Milton family moved from Bread Street to
the western suburb of HAMMERSMITH. Of this residence
and its circumstances we know less than about any other
area associated with Milton; until 1949 it was thought
that the move had been directly from Bread Street to
Horton. Like many other suburbs before and since,
Hammersmith had both its permanent inhabitants and its
summer guests; as late as 1647 the Middlesex Sessions
Books refer to a petition for fair rating presented by
"divers citizens of the city of London, who reside in
the liberty or township of Hammersmith onely in sum-
mertyme, and divers others whose constant residence is
all the year in the said place." Possibly the Miltons
had a summer place there before they made it their
home.

In the absence of more complete data, we can ob-
serve some facts which would certainly have been of
interest to the Miltons at the time they made the move
and which may have influenced their decision to leave
London. In June of 1631 had occurred the culmination
of several years of effort on the part of the residents
of Hammersmith. About 1624 they had decided to ask for
a chapel of their own rather than attend the parish
church at Fulham, their nearest neighbor. In a formal

18

petition made by Lord Mulgrave in 1629, the fact was stressed that the distance to the church at Fulham caused "much neglect of resorting unto the Church on Sundays...a great many spending the time appointed for divine service in profane alehouses and other ungodly exercises." As a positive argument, Mulgrave added that "the Town grows populous and enlargeth every year which this good work will more and more further," while "the remoteness of the ⌈Fulham⌋ church will occasion the remove of divers of the inhabitants now residing and myself among other unless we prevail in our petition."

There is some evidence that there may have been Puritan pressure behind this wish for a chapel-of-ease. At any rate, the petition was granted; Hammersmith received a plot of land 150 x 132 feet; the foundation stone was laid on 11 March 1630; and Archbishop Laud consecrated the church on 7 June 1631.

It is at least a coincidence that a resident of Hammersmith and the chief benefactor of the new church was Nicholas Crisp, a former neighbor on Bread Street. Not only did he give a large part of the subscription for the building of the church but he was the donor of many of the accessories, such as a bell and the painted ceiling.

The original church, which the Miltons must have attended, was completely rebuilt in the 1880s. Here the relics of the past postdate the Milton residence, for they are associated with Crisp, who became an ardent royalist, was knighted by Charles I in 1641, and survived to welcome back Charles' son. Crisp died in the year of the Great Fire. His body, originally entombed in St. Mildred's in Bread Street, now lies in the churchyard, while an imposing monument stands just

19

within the north entrance.

(Fletcher, I: 405-14; Parker, I: 119; II: 779; Survey of London, VI: xvii, 24-26; Whitting, 14, 45-48, 57, 65.)

Harefield and Ludlow:

Although evidence is lacking on whether Milton attended the presentation of either of his two masques, "Arcades" at Harefield and "Comus" at Ludlow, he may well have at least visited the sites. Since both works were probably written during the Hammersmith period, and since Ludlow in particular is of great historical interest in its own right, the two places are included here.

> (HAREFIELD is a small village about four miles from Uxbridge, close to Route A412. For directions to Uxbridge, see under Chalfont St. Giles. Bus Nos. 347 and 348 from Uxbridge go through the village; the church is on the east side of the main street, and the site of the manor house is a short distance beyond.)

The original manor house of Harefield, which was destroyed by fire about 1660, was the home of the Countess Dowager of Derby, Alice Spencer Egerton, from 1601 to 1637. Spenser, her kinsman, had dedicated his "Teares of the Muses" to her, and it was in her honor that Milton's "Arcades" was presented here, probably in 1633.

Situated on a grassy hillside covered with trees, the manor commanded a good view of the surrounding countryside. When Queen Elizabeth had visited Harefield in 1602, she had been greeted by maskers underneath an avenue of elm trees, and some of the allusions in "Arcades" seem to reflect such a particular situation:

20

> O'er the smooth enamell'd green
>
> Where no print of step hath been,
>
> . . . .
>
> Under the shady roof
>
> Of branching Elm Star-proof, ... (11.84-89)

The church contains a marble effigy of the
Countess, in crimson robes and with a gilt coronet,
under a canopy of pale green. The effigies of three
daughters are shown in relief on the sides of the
monument.

(Demaray, 53-55; Esdaile, 19; Masson, I: 566; Parker,
II: 755-58; Roscoe, 6-7.)

> (LUDLOW is about thirty miles northwest
> of Worcester, which is close to M5 or
> A44. It is accessible by British Rail
> by an indirect route from London:
> Worcester is about two and a half hours
> from London, with several trains a
> day; from Worcester one can take a
> train to Hereford and from Hereford to
> Ludlow. Each of these stages takes less
> than an hour, and connections are fairly
> good, but there are only a few trains a
> day, so it is best to plan an overnight
> stay either in Ludlow itself or in
> Worcester. Worcester has many inter-
> esting associations with the Common-
> wealth period, though not directly with
> Milton. Ludlow can also be reached by
> bus from Shrewsbury, Hereford, or
> Birmingham.)

Whether or not Milton attended the first performance of his masque, "Comus," at LUDLOW in September
1634, the town and the Castle are worth a visit. Ly-
ing about twenty-four miles north of Hereford on the
slopes of a hill near the junction of two small rivers
whose waters reach the Severn nearby, the town

Ludlow Castle. Reproduced by permission of the
British Tourist Authority.

supported the Yorkists during the Wars of the Roses and was especially favored by Edward IV. He sent his infant son, Edward, Prince of Wales, to reside there in 1472, and here the boy was proclaimed Edward V on the death of his father, before he and his brother left Ludlow at the summons of their usurping uncle, Richard III. Arthur, son of Henry VII, was also sent here for his education. Upon Arthur's death in 1502 the government of Wales and the Marches was vested in a presidency and council. It was to take up the position of Lord President of Wales that in 1634 John Egerton, Earl of Bridgewater, came to Ludlow and witnessed the masque, for which Henry Lawes, the tutor of his children, had composed the music, and Lawes' friend, John Milton, the words.

The Castle, set at the top of a rocky hill, is still an impressive sight, even though it is in ruins; it must have been magnificent when it was in its prime. By the seventeenth century it included within its great walls a tower, a chapel, and a building used as a jail in the outer bailey, while within the inner bailey were not only the spacious living apartments but kitchens, a keep, a dungeon, and a round Norman chapel, one of the very few of this type known.

The Great Hall, roofless today, was the scene of the performance. It measured sixty feet by thirty. Against the east wall was a dais, with probably a gallery above it. Fastened to the wall in Milton's time were racks holding lances, spears, firelocks, and armor; above the great stone fireplace was a St. Andrew's Cross.

Ludlow Castle served once more as a stronghold during the Civil War, the last garrison in Shropshire

to remain loyal to Charles I; but in 1646 it was forced
to surrender. Four years later Cromwell abolished the
Council of the Marches, and the later Stuarts were un-
successful in an attempt to re-establish it. By the
end of the century the Castle had been leased to the
Earl and Countess of Powis. As late as 1774 many of
the royal apartments were still entire and much of the
furniture, hangings, and other ornaments remained. But
the order of George I that the lead be removed from
the roofs dealt the final blow to the Castle, which by
1811 was in its present state.

(Demaray, 98, 170; Hampton, 9; Masson, Life, I: 570-73.)

1635-1638: HORTON

(HORTON is a short distance off the A4
Road, about seventeen miles west of
London and not far from Windsor. It can
be reached by bus from the nearby town
of Slough. Slough is on the route of
Bus No. 81 as well as most of the Green
Line buses for Windsor; it is served also
by British Rail. The bus from Slough to
Horton runs two or three times a day.
Since the parish church, where Milton's
mother is buried, may be locked, advance
inquiry is advisable; but since the parish has no resident vicar, the best pro-
cedure is to write to the Caretaker of
the church (St. Michael's). The church
is on the right side of the road, coming
from Slough, a short distance beyond the
crossroads and the large tree at the village center. The site of the manor is
almost directly across the road from the
church.)

When the Miltons moved to HORTON, probably in
1635, Milton was in his thirties but still, apparently,
undecided as to a career. At any rate, he was working

24

hard at the intellectual foundations of whatever the career was to be, reading widely and organizing his notes from his reading, interrupting his self-imposed tasks only to compose "Lycidas" (in November 1637).

Then, as now, Horton was a small and peaceful village, about seventeen miles west of London. The neighboring village of Colnbrook, about a mile away, lay on the main highway between London and the West; it would have had shops and inns but apparently was never very important: it has no separate manorial history of its own. The most important house in Horton was the manor house of the Bulstrodes, one of the leading families in the county. The Milton house stood almost opposite the church, where the property still known as Berkin Manor was later erected. The older house was pulled down about 1798.

At least the surroundings and the scenery are authentic. From the large tree at a crossroads one can walk down the road and view the same hills and valleys, if not the identical trees and flowers, which Milton could see. The church, St. Michael's, is not greatly changed, aside from some rebuilding of the south aisle and of the chancel and vestry in the nineteenth century. The nave dates from the middle of the twelfth century, the north transept and the west tower from the fifteenth. The fabric is largely of flint and stone, with some brick in the tower.

Besides its intrinsic interest as an old country church which Milton must have entered many times, it has a special focus of interest for the Miltonist: the grave of Milton's mother, Sara Jeffrey Milton, who died in 1637 and was buried in the chancel of the church. The visitor may stand, as Milton must have stood, beside the plain blue slab with the simple inscription:

25

"Heare lyeth the Body of Sara Milton the wife of John
Milton who Died the 3rd of April, 1637." Almost exact-
ly a year later Milton left Horton for a tour on the
Continent.

(Masson, "Local Memories," 44; Life, I: 506, 594,
Page, History of Buckinghamshire, III: 248, 284-85;
Parker, I: 145; Todd, 23.)

> (LANGLEY, two miles north of Horton,
> can be reached by bus from Slough or
> directly by British Rail or Green
> Line Bus from London; all of these
> run at frequent intervals. Again, it
> is advisable to make arrangements in
> advance, with the Vicar of the Church
> of St. Mary. From the station area,
> turn right on a main street which will
> soon bend to the left; the church is a
> little beyond the bend, on the left
> side of the street; vicarage across
> the road.)

A short distance from Horton is the little town
of LANGLEY. There is no documentary evidence of a
Miltonic connection with it, but the conjecture that
he did make use of the rather unusual library in its
parish church of St. Mary the Virgin has a high degree
of probability.

A prominent feature of the church is the elaborate
Kidderminster pew in the south transept. In the 1620s
a library was built just south of the pew as a result
of a benefaction from Sir John Kidderminster. The
library, entered from the southern side of the pew, re-
sembles it in design. The walls are wainscoted and
painted with various designs, including country scenes
(views of Windsor and Eton and others unidentified),
coats of arms, and various saints. The books, about
250 in number, are in wainscoted presses painted like
the rest of the wall.

Kidderminster had donated the library in 1623 and left further books in his will, which was proved on 7 May 1631. He designed his gift "for the benefit as well of members of the said town [that is, Langley] and such other in the county of Bucks [sic] as resort thereto." The collection includes an eleventh century copy of the Gospels written in England, a fifteenth century printed missal, and many writings of the Church Fathers as well as those of theological writers of the sixteenth and seventeenth centuries. There is a catalog, on vellum, dated 1638. The collection, apparently, was considered complete after the death of Sir John, and someone worked on cataloguing it during the next few years.

Milton's residence at Horton, from (probably) 1635 until he left for Italy in April 1638 was a period of intensive reading. He had begun the systematic notes from at least some of his reading, which had a heavy concentration on patristics and ecclesiastical history. Undoubtedly he owned some books himself, but certainly not all which he read. It seems highly likely that he often took the brief walk from Horton to consult or borrow some of the books which are still treasured in the Kidderminster Library.

(Page, History of Buckinghamshire, III: 246-48, 298-300; Shorter, Highways, 257.)

1639-1640: ST. BRIDE'S CHURCHYARD

(ST. BRIDE'S CHURCH is on the south
side of Fleet Street, just off
Ludgate Circus, a short distance
southwest of St. Paul's. The closest
underground station is Blackfriars,
on the Circle and District lines;
from the station walk north on New
Bridge Street, then left on Fleet.
Bus Nos. 4, 6, 9, 11, 15, 502, and 513
run along Fleet Street.)

Soon after he returned from Italy in the summer of
1639 Milton took lodgings in London with a tailor, Mr.
Russell, in the churchyard of ST. BRIDE'S; this would
have probably been late in 1639 or early in 1640. He
stayed here only a short time, but the place has interest for us because it was his first independent
lodging, because it was here that he began to teach his
nephews, John and Edward Phillips, and because it was
here that he wrote his "Epitaphium Damonis", a lament
for his deceased friend Charles Diodati and the most
important of his Latin poems. The house, which was
very small, burned down in 1824. It was just west of
the church, off the passage down which the tower of St.
Bride's is still seen from Fleet Street. The office of
Punch was on the site for many years.

The church itself was not remarkable in Milton's
time but is of great interest to the modern visitor.
Postwar excavations revealed a Roman ditch and a pave-
ment of a Roman building, both of the first century,
A.D.; the remains of a Saxon cemetery; and remains of
earlier churches on the site going back to the eighth
century. (A description of the early artifacts now in
the crypt will be found in Chapter III.) The churches
of the eighth and twelfth centuries re-used Roman

28

material in their construction, and Wren in turn re-used material from the medieval church; so its fabric incorporated sixteen hundred years of history. St. Bride's suffered a good deal of damage in 1940, however. The spire remained intact, and the rest of the church has been restored.

Milton's work as a polemicist makes it appropriate that his first adult residence was in the heart of a publishing area. Caxton's successor, Wynkyn de Worde, had in 1500 moved his press from the precincts of West-minster Abbey to the area near St. Bride's, drawn there perhaps by its proximity to the many ecclesiastical es-tablishments which contained his best customers. Other printers soon set themselves up in the area, and the career of Fleet Street had begun.

De Worde was buried in St. Bride's, and the Guild of St. Bride's was directed in his will to attend his funeral. Other figures prominent in the literary or newspaper world, among them Samuel Pepys and Samuel Richardson, were later buried there.

It is appropriate, too, that Areopagitica, Milton's best known prose work, published in 1644, dealt with freedom of the press; and that, many years later, after his death, one of his principal publishers, Tonson, had his establishment in Fleet Street.

(French, Life Records, II: 6; Hare, I: 120; Illustrated London News, 223; 1063; Lang, 116; Morgan, 55, 61, 64, 108, 164; Parker, I: 186; Rossiter, 211; Thornbury, II: 220.)

1640-1645: ALDERSGATE STREET

(ALDERSGATE STREET begins slightly north
of St. Paul's Underground Station, Central line. The Barbican station, on
Circle and Metropolitan lines, is near
the northern end of the street, which
is traversed by Bus Nos. 4 and 279A.)

Some time in 1640, probably in the autumn, Milton
rented a large house with a garden in ALDERSGATE STREET,
which stretches northward from St. Martin's le Grand,
near St. Paul's, to just beyond Bridgewater Square.
The name came from a gate built in the city wall in
the ninth century by a Saxon named Aldred or Aldrich.
The gate had been rebuilt in 1618, with a statue of
James I above the central arch, commemorating the fact
that he was the first Stuart king to enter the City by
way of that gateway. It was adorned also with statues
of Samuel and Jeremiah, with scriptural texts. Removed in 1761, its site is now marked by a plaque on
the right side of the street, just above Gresham
Street.

The Aldersgate Street Area. From a map prepared by
Richard Newcourt the elder and engraved by William
Faithorne, published in 1658. Reproduced by permis-
sion of the London Topographical Society and the Map
Division, The New York Public Library, Astor, Lenox
and Tilden Foundations.
   Note especially St. Botolph's Church and Little
Britain (near where the word "Alder" appears) and
Cripplegate in the upper right. Milton's Aldersgate
Street residence was on the right side of the street,
slightly north of Little Britain; Jewin was the first
street above, and Barbican the next above that, approximately where the present Beech Street continues
east from Long Lane.

The locality must have been a pleasant one. It was described in 1657 as resembling an Italian street more than any other in London, "by reason of the spaciousness and uniformity of buildings, and straightness thereof, with the convenient distance of the houses; on both sides whereof there are divers fair ones.... Then is there from about the middle of Aldersgate Street, a handsome new street [Jewin Street] butted out, and fairly built by the Company of Goldsmiths, which reacheth athwart as far as Redcross Street." Among the great houses on Aldersgate Street was the London residence of the Nevilles, while Northumberland House was just below, in St. Martin's le Grand. Quite close to Milton's residence was the large building variously known as Thanet House or Shaftesbury House, built in the 1640s by Inigo Jones and demolished only in 1882. From its first owners, the Earls of Thanet, it passed to Anthony Ashley Cooper, afterwards Earl of Shaftesbury (the Achitophel of Dryden's poem). At the beginning of the eighteenth century it reverted to the possession of the Thanet family. Later it was successively an inn, a hospital, and a dispensary.

In the nineteenth century it was possible to identify the exact site not only of this first Aldersgate Street house but of Milton's later residences in Jewin Street and Barbican. Today, however, the great Barbican development has swallowed up the streets on the eastern side, and all landmarks have disappeared. The house must have stood just north of the present London Museum. Masson was able to reconstruct the position of the house in relation to its surroundings: the garden, quite spacious, lay in front, opening from a passageway in Aldersgate Street, the house itself occupying the southeast corner of the garden area, with a side entrance from another street.

About Milton's life at this period many details
are known, and the reasons for his moving here are evi-
dent. He needed space for his books and furniture, and
he was now adding other pupils to his two nephews, so
the St. Bride's lodgings were inadequate. The household at Horton seems to have broken up about this time:
Christopher was married and living in Reading, where
the father joined him. Milton, no doubt pleased with
the relative spaciousness as well as the privacy and
quiet (for the house stood back from the street at the
end of an entry), settled down to the life of a
scholar-teacher.

In neither role were his expectations completely
fulfilled. A scholar he remained, but his writings
could not be the leisurely, un-pressured productions
which he envisioned, since from 1641 on he was drawn
into the controversial writing which was to occupy him
for almost twenty years. He continued to teach his
nephews, but the other pupils dwindled away. The
earliest biographer implies that "the tempers of our
Gentry would not beare the strictness of his Discipline," while his nephew testifies that Milton himself gave "an Example to those under him ... of hard
Study, and spare Diet; ..."

It was fortunate, however, that the house was
large, for to it soon came other residents. The Civil
War had broken out; Reading had surrendered to the
Parliamentary forces on 27 April 1643; Christopher, a
Royalist, had gone to Wells and Exeter to work for the
royal party, and the elder Mr. Milton, now almost
eighty, came to live with Milton. A few months later
Milton returned from the country a married man,

33

bringing with him his bride, Mary Powell, and a number
of her relatives, who seem to have remained for several
weeks. As all the world knows, it was not long before
Mary herself left to visit her mother in Forest Hill
and, at the end of the visit, declined to return. When
a reconciliation was effected in 1645, it took place
at the home of Milton's relatives, William and Hester
Blackborough, in the nearby street of St. Martin's le
Grand (known before the Fire as St. Martin's Lane).

The period at Aldersgate Street is notable for
Milton's first major prose works. Beginning with Of
Reformation in England in 1641, several anti-episcopal
and divorce tracts were published before 1645, in-
cluding The Reason of Church Government Urged Against
Prelaty and The Doctrine and Discipline of Divorce.
Of Education and Areopagitica were also the products
of these years. Poetry was represented by some topical
sonnets. Of exceptional interest is one written in
November 1642, "When the Assault Was Intended to the
City," for it refers to this very house; the original
title, in the Trinity MS, was "On his door when the
City expected an assault." London at this time was in
momentary fear of attack from the Royalist forces.
Milton, wholeheartedly for the Parliamentary cause,
had made the decision to defend it by the pen rather
than the sword. It was his hope that his status as a
poet would raise him above partisan politics and that
the value of his poetic gift might be appreciated. He
recalls historical episodes when a conqueror had
spared a poet's dwelling and pleads for a similar con-
sideration for his own home. Whether he is writing
seriously or playfully may be debated, but in any case
the reference is clear:

> Captain or Colonel, or Knight in Arms,
>> Whose chance on these defenseless
>>> doors may seize,
>> If ever deed of honor did these please,
>> Guard them, and him within protect
>>> from harms;
> He can requite thee, for he knows the charms
>> That call Fame on such gentle acts
>>> as these,
>> And he can spread thy Name o'er Lands
>>> and Seas,
>> Whatever clime the Sun's bright circle
>>> warms.
> Lift not thy spear against the Muses' Bow'r:
>> The great Emathian Conqueror bid spare
>> The house of Pindarus, when Temple
>>> and Tow'r
>> Went to the ground; and the repeated air
>> Of sad Electra's Poet had the pow'r
>> To save th' Athenian Walls from ruin bare.

(Bush, 52; French, Life Records, II: 9-10; Masson, "Local Memories," 131-33; Parker, I: 192, 230-34; Smith, 13; Wheatley, I: 22-23, II: 486.)

St. Botolph's Church:

On the left side of Aldersgate Street is ST. BOTOLPH'S CHURCH, which was Milton's parish during the five years of his residence here. St. Botolph was a Saxon saint known as the patron of wayfarers, so a dedication to him was frequent near gates. The church was hardly touched by the Great Fire but had to be taken down in 1790. A few relics and monuments, however, survive. When the new church was built the east

wall was merely heightened. The communion table dates
from 1639. Alexander Gill, the headmaster of St.
Paul's School, was buried here in 1642, and Milton may
well have attended this and the funerals of other
friends.

The modern visitor will be interested in the
series of windows on the south side, each of which com-
memorates a historical event associated with the neighborhood; William I conferring the patronage of St.
Botolph's on the Dean of the priory of St. Martin's le
Grand; James I entering the City by Aldersgate; Compton,
the Bishop of London, giving shelter to Princess Anne
in 1688; and Wesley preaching in Moorfields in 1738.

(London City Churches, 10; Norman, 2; Thornbury, II:
221; Wheatley, I: 226.)

Forest Hill:

> (FOREST HILL is a few miles east of
> Oxford, near Route A40. A bus (No. 280)
> runs frequently from Oxford, covering
> the distance in fifteen or twenty min-
> utes. There are few landmarks, but the
> bus driver will let you off at a small
> country road, leading to the left. The
> church (St. Nicholas) is a short dis-
> tance up a hill on the left side of the
> lane. The church may be locked; the
> vicarage is nearby. The Powell home
> was a little beyond the church on the
> same side of the lane.)

Milton's first wife, Mary Powell, lived in FOREST
HILL, a village five or six miles east of Oxford.
Milton's month-long residence there in 1642 is referred
to by Edward Phillips in a well-known passage: "About
Whitsuntide it was, or a little after, that he took a

Journey into the Country; no body about him certainly
knowing the Reason, or that it was any more than a
Journey of Recreation: after a Month's stay, home he
returns a Married-man, that went out a Batchelor; his
Wife being <u>Mary</u>, the Eldest Daughter of Mr. <u>Richard
Powell</u>, then a Justice of Peace, of <u>Forrest-hil</u>, near
<u>Shotover</u> in <u>Oxfordshire</u>."

Richard Powell, Mary's father, lived in a sizable
and well-furnished house of which some authentic

Forest Hill. The manor house which was the home of Mary
Powell. Drawing by Karen McCann from a sketch in
Robert Chambers' <u>Cyclopedia of American Literature</u>
(Philadelphia, 1849).

details are known. It had fourteen rooms, in addition
to a kitchen, bakehouse, dairy, and other small working
areas; an inventory made a few years after Mary left
there includes carpets, cushions, pictures, embroidered
chairs, etc., which suggest a commodious household.
The original manor house was torn down in 1854; a picture of it survives, and the site, quite close to the
church, is known.

In the church, presumably, the wedding took place,
probably in the early summer of 1642. It is an attrac-
tive stone church with a bell-tower. The buttresses
which shore it up were built in 1639 and must have been
white and new when the wedding took place. Between the
church and the site of the manor house is a gateway
which dates from the period, and nearby is a mounting
block which is also very old.

(Darishire, 63; French, <u>Life Records</u>, II: 62; Masson,
<u>Life</u>, II; 501; Parker, II: 872; Rowse, 95, 110.)

1645-1647: BARBICAN

(As a result of rebuilding after World
War II, the name "Barbican" is now
given to a large area bounded by Aldersgate Street on the west, Beech Street
and Chiswell Street on the north, Moor
Lane on the east, Fore Street and London
Wall on the south. Almost all the former streets within the present complex
have disappeared. In Milton's day
BARBICAN was a street running east from
Aldersgate. The directions given for
reaching Aldersgate Street apply also to
Barbican.)

At about the same time that the reconciliation
with his wife had been effected, Milton was planning to

Milton's house in Barbican as it was in the nineteenth
century. Drawing by Karen McCann from a sketch in
David Masson's In the Footsteps of the Poets (New
York, 1894).

move to a still larger house in a street called the
BARBICAN. Mary stayed for a short time with Christopher
Milton's mother-in-law in St. Clement's Churchyard;
Parker speculates plausibly that this temporary arrange-
ment was made in view of the fact that the new house
would soon be ready and that it might be easier to
make a fresh start in new surroundings. This hypothesis
fits the facts reported by Phillips, Milton's nephew:
it was decided that Milton's wife "should remain at a
Friend's house, till such time as he was settled in
his New house at <u>Barbican</u>, and all things for her
reception in order."

To Barbican, then, the family moved in the fall of
1645. The street took its name from a Roman tower
which had stood just to the north; in Saxon times
fires were lighted on the top of the tower to guide
travelers through the hills of Hampstead and Highgate
to the city gates. The new home was only a few min-
utes' walk from the old: Barbican ran east from
Aldersgate approximately where Beech Street now is.
One who stands on the south side of Bridgewater Square
(where the Earl of Bridgewater had his town house) and
looks south into the new Barbican project will be close
to the original site.

This house survived long enough to be seen by
Masson in the nineteenth century and to be pictured
in the <u>Illustrated London News</u> of 16 July, 1864, at
about which date it was destroyed to make way for the
Metropolitan Railway. It was a brick house with bay
windows, with a rather narrow frontage but considerably
wider at the back, and had a large garden space.

When the Metropolitan Railway needed the site in
the 1860s, the land was valued at two hundred and six

pounds a year. There was, understandably, however, a dispute over the real value, and eventually a jury awarded compensation of more than three thousand pounds.

One or two rather strange relics of this building remain for the curious. A fragment of brick from the house was presented to Yale College by Moses C. Tyler; it is still preserved in the Yale University Library. A pane of glass from the house is supposed to have been sent to Toledo, Ohio, but no trace of this has been found by modern researchers.

During the two years that Milton resided here some important events in his life took place. These included the birth of his first child, Anne, in the summer of 1646, and the death of his father in March 1647. In the meantime, Oxford had surrendered to the Parliamentarians in June 1646, and the whole Powell family (the mother and father of Mary with several of their children) came to live with Milton. The father, Richard Powell, died in January 1647, and the other members of the family probably dispersed to other refuges during the summer of that year.

At the end of 1645 appeared the volume of Milton's Poems which included most of what he had written up to this point; but these two years, understandably, were not very productive from a literary point of view. There were pupils to be taught; the house was crowded and no doubt noisy; the political situation was disturbed. Two sonnets, however, can be definitely dated to 1646: "To My Friend, Mr. Henry Lawes, on His Airs," and the one written in memory of Mrs. Catharine Thomason, who died in December 1646. It is possible, of course, that Milton was doing some

41

work on _Paradise Lost_ and on some of the prose which
was finished or published later.

(_Athenaeum_, 5 Nov. 1864, p. 603; French, _Life Records_,
II: 128-29, 173; Masson, "Local Memories," 135, _Life_,
III: 443-44; Parker, I: 288, 299, 303-304; Smith, 19.)

1647-1649: HIGH HOLBORN

(The house in HOLBORN, near LINCOLN'S
INN FIELDS, was probably in the area
of Whetstone Park, a short street just
south of Holborn Underground station
on Central and Piccadilly lines, east
of Kingsway and parallel with the
northern side of Lincoln's Inn Square.
Bus Nos. 8, 22, 25 and 501 run along
Holborn.

The church of St. Giles in the Fields
is at the western end of High Holborn
near its junction with Charing Cross
Road and Tottenham Court Road. The
Tottenham Court Road station (Central
and Northern lines) is at this junction.
Nearby buses are Nos. 14, 19, 24, 29,
38, and 176.)

In the fall of 1647 Milton moved again, this time
to a smaller house, in HOLBORN, near LINCOLN'S INN
FIELDS. His father had died; he no longer had the
Powell relatives with him; and possibly some of his
pupils had gone on to the university.

Holborn was a main thoroughfare, important enough
to have been partly paved as early as 1535. Though it
underwent some modification at its eastern extremity
with the construction of Holborn Viaduct in the nineteenth century, its route has not changed. Leading
eastward from New Oxford Street at Drury Lane, it is
known as High Holborn until it reaches Chancery Lane;
from there to Fetter Lane it is Holborn; and from

Fetter Lane to Farringdon Street it is continued by Holborn Viaduct, formerly Holborn Hill.

Milton's house was on the south side of High Holborn, backing on Lincoln's Inn Fields, betweenGreat and Little Turnstiles. A small street called Whetstone Park lies in the area described, between the north side of Lincoln's Inn Fields and the south side of High Holborn; Milton's house must have been about here.

No trace of the house has survived, but about Lincoln's Inn Fields we know a good deal, so that it is not difficult to recover an idea of the surroundings. The neat park of today has had a long history. During the reign of Elizabeth I the fields were pasture grounds in the hands of the Crown. In 1617 there was a petition to James I from the gentlemen of the Inns of Court and Chancery and from the four parishes adjoining the fields that they be converted into walks, as Moorfields had recently been. The conversion of the open fields into "faire and goodlye walkes, would be a matter of greate ornament to the Citie, pleasure and freshnes for the health and recreation of the Inhabitantes thereabout, and for the sight and delight of Embassadors and Strangers coming to our Court and Citie, and a memorable worke of our tyme to all posteritie." Inigo Jones was one of the commissioners chosen for the undertaking, which apparently had some success. But the projected benefits were jeopardized when in 1638 a William Newton received permission to do some building. The Society of Lincoln's Inn protested, asserting that the buildings would deprive them of fresh air, annoy them with unpleasant smells, and cause other inconveniences, to their great discouragement and the disquieting of their studies.

Newton, however, went ahead with his building operations, apparently realizing some of the fears of the protesters, for in 1645 another petition complained that many thousand loads of dung and dirt had been laid in the fields, and a common horse pool made therein, so that nearby residents were "almost quite deprived of their former liberty of Walking, Training, drying of Cloathes, and recreating themselves in the said fields." Eventually a compromise was reached, the Society of Lincoln's Inn declaring that it did not object to buildings along the sides of the fields, as long as the prospect and the air were maintained.

This background helps to clarify the well-known "Prospect of Lincoln's Inn Fields" published by Wenceslas Hollar a few years before Milton moved into the area. The elegance of the houses in Hollar's view is not belied by the one example that remains: Lindsey House, no. 59 and 60, on the west side of Lincoln's Inn Square. This may have been designed by Inigo Jones himself, under whose influence most of the houses on the square were done. The exterior is of stone and brick (part of the front was stuccoed and painted at a later period); Ionic pilasters, resting on pedestals, decorate the walls; and the courtyard is adorned with brick piers.

The most important domestic event of the period spent in this house was the birth of Milton's second daughter, Mary, in October 1648. There may have been some disappointment that it was not a boy; certainly there was worry at the time about Milton's failing eyesight; and the political situation was rapidly deteriorating. Conditions were not favorable to literary composition. Nevertheless, Milton's translations of

Psalms 80 to 88 date from this period, as well as the sonnet on Fairfax, with its memorable line, "For what can War, but endless war still breed, . . ." He was probably working on the History of Britain: and towards the end of the period he wrote the first salvo in the campaign designed to prove to the public, English and European, the righteousness of the Parliamentary cause: The Tenure of Kings and Magistrates, published early in 1649.

(Barker and Jackson, 118-19; French, Life Records, II: 199-200; Harben, 303; Hayes, London: A Pictorial History, no. 37; Parker, I: 312, 347; Survey of London, III: 8-12, 96-97; Thornbury, III: 50; Wheatley, II: 219-20, III: 490.)

St. Giles in the Fields:

Mary was baptized on 7 November 1648 in the Church of ST. GILES IN THE FIELDS. In the seventeenth century -- indeed, until New Oxford Street was cut through in 1847 -- it stood on the only main road to the West except the Strand. It was still largely a country area and was beginning to be very fashionable. The church, originally a leper hospital founded by Queen Maud in 1177, had been rebuilt in the 1620s and consecrated by Laud in 1630. Most of its rich ornaments, however, had been sold in 1643 as a result of the protest of parishioners against the "superstitious and idolatrous" practices of the incumbent.

(French, Life Records, II: 220; Jenkinson, 251, 290; Survey of London, V: 127-30; Trent, 82.)

1649-1651: CHARING CROSS AND WHITEHALL

(CHARING CROSS and WHITEHALL are both just off Trafalgar Square. The Under-

ground station, now called Charing
Cross, is on Northern, Bakerloo,
and Jubilee lines, and numerous
buses converge on Trafalgar Square.
Spring Gardens is just outside the
Admiralty Arch, on the southwest of
the Square. Great Scotland Yard
branches off to the right as one
goes down Northumberland Avenue,
from the southeast part of the Square.)

Of all Milton's residences, those at CHARING
CROSS and WHITEHALL are the most difficult to picture
today, since the Trafalgar Square area where they were
located has changed so drastically. We do know, however, their approximate location.

After his appointment as Secretary for Foreign
Tongues in February 1649, Milton soon took temporary
lodgings "at one Thomson's, next door to the Bull Head
Tavern at Charing Cross, opening into the Spring Garden." The Cross itself had stood somewhat west of the
location of its present replica; it was approximately
where the statue of Charles I now stands. Another symbol of idolatry, it had been destroyed by Puritans in
1647 (although it appears that Londoners in general
missed the old landmark: in an amusing ballad of the
period they pretend puzzlement at its absence:

The Whitehall area. From the Newcourt-Faithorne map of
1658. Reproduced by permission of the London Topographical Society and the Map Division, The New York Public
Library, Astor, Lenox and Tilden Foundations.
Milton's residence from 1649 to 1651 was first in
Spring Garden (to the left of Charing Cross) and then
in Scotland Yard (upper right). Petty France, where he
lived from 1651 to 1660, ran parallel to the southern
edge of St. James' Park, near the lower left of the map.

At the end of the Strand they make a stand,
Swearing they are at a loss;
And chafing say, "This is not the way:
We must go by Charing Cross.")

There is still a small street named Spring Garden
just outside the Admiralty Arch, at the southwest corner of the Square. The Garden, a popular spot for
ladies and gallants, had housed an ordinary and bowling
green under Charles I, but these were closed by Cromwell, to be reopened after the Restoration. Close by
was the home of Sir Harry Vane, a Parliamentary leader
particularly admired by Milton. When Milton lived
there it must have been decent enough, since in 1647 an
ordinance had been passed directing that the keeper of
Spring Garden not admit any person to come into or walk
there on the Lord's Day or any public fast day; and that
no wine, beer, ale, cakes, or other things be sold there
on those days.

As soon as it could be arranged, though that was
not until November of 1649, Milton moved from his temporary lodgings into Whitehall itself. The so-called
Palace of Whitehall was in reality a conglomeration of
many different buildings erected at different times,
joined by irregular courtyards and narrow passages. It
contained 2000 rooms for officials, courtiers, and
royalty. Cromwell and his officials had by this time
taken it over.

Milton's apartment was in Scotland Yard, at the
northern end of Whitehall Palace, near the southeast
corner of what is now Trafalgar Square. Originally the
site of a palace built by the Saxon kings for the reception of the kings of Scotland when they visited, it was
by the time of Elizabeth I in bad condition and in any

case no longer served its original purpose after the union of Scotland and England. It had therefore been remodeled and now served for the use of government officials. The present Great Scotland Yard, which joins Northumberland Avenue with Whitehall (the street), marks this site.

The apartment was certainly convenient because of its proximity to the Council, with which Milton evidently worked closely. It may have been less comfortable than the "pretty garden houses" which were usually his choice. There is a record of his being granted by the Council some hangings from the late King's goods; this was several months after he took up residence.

During this period Milton produced two of his most important prose works, Eikonoklastes, in reply to the Royalist Eikon Basilike, and the First Defense of the English People.

In Whitehall, on 16 March 1651, Milton's third child, the first son, was born, and named John, like his father and grandfather. In January of that year a Committee for Whitehall had been told to examine the list of occupants and make changes; more room was needed for members of Parliament (and one wonders whether the bureaucracy was growing). By spring Milton was definitely in danger of being ousted; but the Council intervened and asked Parliament to let Mr. Milton remain, since it was very helpful to them to have him near.

(Barker and Jackson, 132; French, Life Records, II: 237, 273-74; 314; Knight, I: 191-92; Masson, "Local Memories," 137; Life, IV: 107; Mead, 99; Parker, I: 359-61, 378, II: 961, 966; Thornbury, III: 330, IV: 77.)

1651-1660: PETTY FRANCE

(PETTY FRANCE, which reverted to its
older name after many years of existence
as York Place, runs east from Buckingham
Gate; it is a short distance south of St.
James Park, parallel with the western
half of Birdcage Walk. The St. James
Park Underground Station, Circle and
District lines, is close to its eastern extremity. No direct bus service,
but it is within walking distance of
any of the buses that run along
Parliament Street, near Westminster.)

But by the end of 1651 Milton did vacate his
Whitehall apartment. His new home was in PETTY FRANCE.
In a letter written on the last day of the year, he
speaks of the move as "necessary and sudden..., because
of my health." A new Parliamentary committee may have
been exerting pressure again, and certainly his eyesight was failing, so there was ample reason for him to
take up what he probably hoped would be a permanent
residence and in which, as a matter of fact, he remained for more than eight years. He may have rented
it from Dr. Nathan Paget, who some years later was to
recommend his cousin, Elizabeth Minshull, as Milton's
third wife.

The new house was within easy walking distance of
the Whitehall offices. The street was called Petty
France, from the fact that it had once been populated
by French residents; the name was changed to York
Place at the time of the French Revolution but is now
again known by its former name. The garden of the
house opened on St. James' Park, which during the
reigns of Elizabeth and the first two Stuarts was
largely a nursery for deer; James I had installed a
menagerie of exotic animals. Next door to Milton lived
Lord Scudamore who, as ambassador to Paris in 1638, had

50

Milton's house in Petty France. Drawing by Karen McCann from a sketch in David Masson's <u>In the Footsteps of the Poets</u> (New York, 1894).

welcomed Milton there, introduced him to Grotius, and facilitated his journey into Italy.

One can still enter Petty France from Queen Anne's Gardens and find the site of Milton's house somewhat less than halfway down the street on the right. A better idea can actually be obtained by going along Birdcage Walk, which skirts the southern edge of the Park, and looking across from about where the Wellington Barracks now stand; for there was an entrance on the garden side, which opened directly into the Park. It was a pleasant neighborhood, and the house, too, about which we have a good deal of information, was very livable. It was built of red brick and had three floors, with many windows on each floor.

Before the house was demolished in 1875, again to make way for the Metropolitan Railway, it had had other distinguished inhabitants. In the early part of the nineteenth century it belonged to Jeremy Bentham and was rented by John Mill, the father of John Stuart Mill, then a small child. Bentham had placed on the house a tablet with the inscription "Sacred to Milton, Prince of Poets," and he is said to have made visitors kneel before it. A little later the house was occupied for several years by William Hazlitt. Coventry Patmore, who visited Hazlitt there, described the wall near the chimney as "covered by names written in pencil, of all sizes and characters, and in all directions, commemorative of visits of curiosity to the house of ... [John Milton]."

The Historical Society of Pennsylvania owns a relic of this house: a balustrade pillar composed of four twisted columns presented by Bentham in 1821 to Richard Rush, at the time Envoy to Britain. The same

Society has a watercolor sketch of the house and garden as they were in 1821. Another interesting relic is a copy of the first edition of <u>Paradise Lost</u> bound in boards taken from a rafter in the house.

Milton's fourth child and third daughter, Deborah, was born here in May 1652. But the personal memories associated with the house are almost uniformly sad. In the first year of his residence there his wife died, a few days after having given birth to Deborah. Less than two months later the baby John, fifteen months old, also died; and in the same year Milton's blindness became total. During the first part of the decade he continued to work for the Commonwealth and the Protectorate; towards the end he was forced to realize, although he clung to hope until the last moment, that the cause for which he had sacrificed so much was doomed.

In November 1656 he married a second time. His wife was the twenty-eight-year-old Katherine Woodcock, who bore him a daughter in October 1657; but the child lived only until the following March, and Katherine herself had died in February, after a little less than fifteen months of marriage.

Despite the personal sorrows which marked the eight years of Milton's residence in Petty France, he must have been gratified by the marks of esteem which he there received. Many distinguished visitors came to see him: Lady Ranelagh, whose sons he had instructed; friends like Andrew Marvell, Marchamont Needham, Edward Lawrence, to whom a sonnet was written, and Cyriack Skinner, also the recipient of two sonnets. In addition, there were visitors from abroad; Phillips speaks of the visits of "all Learned Foreigners of Note, who could not part out of this City, without giving a visit to a person so Eminent."

The period is represented in poetry by a second group of Psalm translations (1 to 8, made in 1653) and by several sonnets, including some of those best known: "To the Lord General Cromwell"; the tribute to Sir Henry Vane; "On the Late Massacre in Piemont"; "When I consider how my light is spent"; and "Methought I saw my late espoused Saint." Undoubtedly also, with his services for the government curtailed by his blindness, he was able to turn at last to serious work on the great epic which had been germinating for so many years. In prose, he may have been working on the History of Britain and the Christian Doctrine. In 1654 the Second Defense of the English People summed up the Cromwellian position and incidentally afforded him an opportunity to record some of the events and attitudes of his own life. In 1659 appeared A Treatise of Civil Power in Ecclesiastical Causes, and in the last desperate days in the spring of 1660 The Ready and Easy Way to Establish a Free Commonwealth urged the nation to make use of its last opportunity for freedom.

(Archer, 10; Barker and Jackson, 130; French, Life Records, III: 109-10, 220-21, 228-29; Knight, I: 190-97; Lang, 340; Masson, "Local Memories," 170-3; Parker, I: 400, 583, II: 999; Westlake, 124.)

Note: The parish church of St. Margaret will be discussed in Chapter II.)

1660: BARTHOLOMEW CLOSE

(BARTHOLOMEW CLOSE is west of Aldersgate
Street, south of Long Lane, near Smithfield. It is about midway between the
Barbican (Circle and Metropolitan) and
St. Paul's (Central) Underground stations. The most convenient route is
probably to walk west on Little Britain
from Aldersgate Street and enter the
Close at the first main intersection (to
the right) after Little Britain veers
north.)

With the Restoration of Charles II and the con-
sequent real danger to Milton, he had to leave the
house in Petty France and take refuge with a friend
(whose name is not known) in BARTHOLOMEW CLOSE. This
was probably early in May 1660.   Here he remained
until the danger was over. On 13 August a proclama-
tion was issued stating that since John Milton had
fled, the only action that could be taken was to call
in and burn his books; and on the twenty-ninth of the
month a general pardon was issued. His stay in the
Close was therefore about four months.

Bartholomew Close was an irregular space occupying
part of the enclosed grounds, or close, of the ancient
Priory. It could be entered by one of several ways:
from West Smithfield, from Little Britain, from Long
Lane, and through Cloth Fair; these are still the entrances today. The area is not very large and the
buildings along the sides of the Close not numerous.
One of them must occupy the site of the home of Milton's
friend.

More than many other parts of modern London, much
of this area brings us close to the atmosphere of the
seventeenth century. Unlike the spacious and carefully
laid out squares which had already begun to be popular,

The Elizabethan gatehouse at the Church of St. Barthol-
omew. Milton took refuge in Bartholomew Close in 1660.
Reproduced by permission of the Rector of the Priory
Church of St. Bartholomew the Great.

this is still a huddle of buildings dominated by the Priory Church of St. Bartholomew, one of the oldest and most interesting of London's churches; actually it is the oldest parochial church now standing in London. Founded as an Augustinian monastery in 1123 by Rahere, a former courtier of Henry I, it was granted at the Dissolution to Sir Richard Rich, who himself resided in the Close. It became at that time the parish church for the district, but most of the monastic buildings as well as the nave of the church were destroyed to make way for developments planned by the new owner. When the King sold the priory, however, the choir of the church and its transepts were granted to the parishioners. These are still one of the most impressive sights in London.

The present square brick tower of the church was erected in 1628. It has five of the oldest bells in London, dating from before 1510; they are dedicated to Saints Bartholomew, Katherine, Anne, John the Baptist, and Peter. From his place of hiding Milton must often have heard their peals.

St. Bartholomew's escaped damage during the Fire and the bombing, so its appearance has remained practically unaltered. The bombing actually added something to the interest of the site, since it exposed a hitherto unsuspected Elizabethan gatehouse, which now dominates the entrance from Smithfield.

In 1660 the Close was already a center for printers, and sixty-five years later Benjamin Franklin worked at a printing house here.

(Archer, 4; Brett-James, 31; Daniell, 37-38; Harben, 49; Masson, Life VI: 162; Wheatley, I: 109.)

1660-1661: RED LION SQUARE

(RED LION SQUARE is not far from
Milton's earlier residence near
Lincoln's Inn Fields but lies north
of High Holborn instead of south.
It is east of Southampton Row and
south of Theobald's Road, very
close to the Holborn Underground
station on Central and Piccadilly
lines. Southampton Row is served
by Bus Nos. 68, 77, 170, 188, and
239; Theobald's Road by 5, 55, 19,
38, and 172.)

After leaving Bartholomew Close Milton stayed for
a short time, perhaps a few months, in RED LION FIELDS,
now Red Lion Square, a short distance from his earlier
home near Lincoln's Inn Fields. Red Lion Fields, a
little north of Holborn, took the name from Red Lion
Inn, which was one of the largest in the district. A
generation later the area was described as a "pleasant
square of good buildings, between High Holborn south,
and the fields north." Since the Square was not fully
developed until about 1684, the fields rather than the
buildings must have been dominant when Milton lived
there.

A tradition recorded by Chancellor and Jesse
(among others) relates that the bodies of Cromwell,
Ireton, and Bradshaw, which were disinterred in January
1661, were brought to the Red Lion Inn, where they remained during the night, before the hanging of the
bodies the following day. One hopes that Milton had
moved before this event occurred. Another tradition
states that the body of Cromwell was re-buried in the
Square, the spot being marked later by an obelisk
erected by one of his admirers. The obelisk remained
until the middle of the nineteenth century.

Today the Square is a quiet and pleasant park.
Dante Gabriel Rossetti, Edward Burne-Jones, and William
Morris all resided there, in a house (No. 17) on the
south side.

(Chancellor, Squares of London, 172-74, 179; Jesse,
124-26; Masson, "Local Memories," 173; Parker, I: 574;
Thornbury, IV: 545, 548.)

1661-1669: JEWIN STREET

(The residence in JEWIN STREET is in
the same general area as those in
Aldersgate Street and Barbican. It
was situated a little farther east.)

Milton's next move was to JEWIN STREET, close to
his former homes in Aldersgate Street and Barbican,
about half-way between them. His residence there began in late 1660 or early 1661 and terminated (if we
follow Parker's dating) eight or nine years later.
Jewin Street ran east from Aldersgate to Redcross
Street. It took its name from the fact that until 1177
this was the only place where the Jews were allowed to
bury their dead. Hence it was the Jews' Garden, eventually Jewin. Like most of the other old streets in
the area, it has disappeared in the Barbican development. All we know about Milton's house is that it
must have been towards the eastern end of the street,
since he was now in the parish of St. Giles Cripplegate
(which will be described in Chapter II).

To the early biographers we owe many details of
Milton's personal and literary life while he lived
here. With political dangers now past, and political

writing impossible, he could at last devote himself to his literary work. Much of _Paradise Lost_ must have been written here. Andrew Marvell, the poet (who may have been instrumental in protecting his friend from punishment at the Restoration) was a frequent visitor, and Thomas Ellwood, a young Quaker admirer, came each day to read to him, since his daughters were unwilling or unable to help their father very much. The most significant personal event, which occurred in February 1663, was his marriage to Elizabeth Minshull, a young and apparently very agreeable woman, with whom he was to live happily for the rest of his days.

The year 1667 marked what is for posterity the most momentous event in Milton's life, the publication of _Paradise Lost_. The contract was signed in April; the publisher was Samuel Simmons, whose establishment was in Aldersgate Street, close to Milton's residence. The author was to receive five pounds at once, with the promise of another five pounds when 1300 copies had been sold, and further payments of five pounds each if a second or third edition of 1300 copies were needed. This historic document is now in the British Museum.

(French, _Life Records_, IV: 354; Hare, I: 266-67; Jesse, I: 338; Parker, I: 601, II: 1089; Wheatley, II: 308.)

(Milton's temporary residence at the village of Chalfont St. Giles from July 1665 to the following February or March is treated in the next chapter.)

1670:   LITTLE BRITAIN

(For directions to LITTLE BRITAIN, see again Aldersgate Street and Barbican.

The street goes off to the left near
the southern end of Aldersgate Street,
just north of St. Botolph's Church,
and opposite the London Museum.)

Before describing Milton's final London residence
it is appropriate to mention LITTLE BRITAIN, where he
lodged for an unspecified length of time with his
friend Edward Millington, a bookseller, some time between 1663 and 1670. Richardson, the only early biographer who mentions this residence, places it between
his references to Jewin Street and Artillery Row and
says that Milton lived here "about 1670." In the absence of conclusive evidence for either date or cir-
cumstance, Parker's conjecture seems reasonable: that
when the move from Jewin Street to a smaller house was
taking place, Milton and his books may have stayed
with his friend while the third Mrs. Milton was getting
the new house ready.

In any case, Little Britain has authentic links
with Milton as well as a long and interesting history
of its own. Its name is traced back either to the
Duke of Brittany who came to England with William the
Conqueror or more probably (according to Ekwall) to a
Robert le Bretoun who in the thirteenth century owned
some houses here. It was known for a while as Duck
Lane, later misinterpreted as Duke; then as Peti Bre-
tane; and finally as Little Britain. From the fifteenth
to the early eighteenth century it was a center of the
book trade; Millington was a seller of old books, at
the sign of the Pelican.

The street follows today the same line -- an
erratic one -- that it did in Milton's day. Running
to the left from Aldersgate Street, just north of St.
Botolph's Church, it goes due west for a short distance

61

and then curves to the northwest, ending as it reaches
the intersection of West Smithfield and Long Lane near
St. Bartholonew's hospital. It was just so that Stow
described it about 1600: "And on this west side of
Aldersgate streete, by S. Buttolphes church is Briton
street, which runneth west to a pumpe, and then north
to the gate, which entreth the churchyeard somtime
pertaining to the Priory of S. Bartholomew, on the east
side: and on the west side towards S. Bartholomewes
spittle, to a paire of postes there fixed."

    During his many residences in the area Milton
must often have walked along this street of booksellers. It was in Little Britain that, one may say,
the reputation of Paradise Lost began. Richardson
tells the story of how the Earl of Dorset, a year or
two after the publication of the poem,

> was in Little-Britain, Beating about
> for Books to his Taste; There was
> Paradise Lost; He was Surpriz'd with
> Some Passages he Struck upon Dipping
> Here and There, and Bought it; the
> Bookseller Begg'd him to speak in its
> Favour if he lik'd it, for that they
> lay on his Hands as Wast Paper. . . .
> My Lord took it Home, Read it, and
> sent it to Dryden, who in a short time
> return'd it: This Man (says Dryden)
> Cuts us All Out, and the Ancients too.

(Darbishire, 75; Ekwall, 85; Parker, I: 608, II: 1127;
Smith, 117, Stow I: 304.)

1669-1674: BUNHILL ROW

62

(To reach BUNHILL ROW: from the Old
Street Underground station on the
Northern line, walk west on Old Street
and turn left on to BUNHILL ROW: or
from Moorgate Station on Central and
Metropolitan lines, walk north on
Moorgate to Finsbury Square (not
Finsbury Circus, which is just outside
the station), then left on Chiswell
Street, right on Bunhill Row. Bus
Nos. 76, 104, 141, 214, and 271 oper-
ate on City Road, just east of Bunhill
Row, between Finsbury Square and Old
Street.)

Milton's last home was located in BUNHILL ROW,
also known as Artillery Walk or Artillery Row. Edward
Phillips relates that ". . .he stay'd not long [in
Jewin Street] after his new Marriage, ere he remov'd
to a House in the Artillery-walk leading to Bunhill
Fields. And this was his last Stage in this World,
. . ." Following Phillips, later biographers have
often supposed that this move took place about 1663,
the year in which Milton married Elizabeth Minshull;
but Parker has argued convincingly (Milton, II: 1125-
26) for a later date, probably 1669 or 1670. At any
rate, it was indeed Milton's last stage in this world.

The house was still in the general area of Aldersgate Street but farther north and east. Variously
known as Artillery Row and Bunhill Row, the street at
the time had houses only on the west side, the other
side being open to the fields. Except that houses now
line most of the east side of the street also, the to-
pography has not changed: the area between Bunhill Row
and what is now the City Road is still occupied by the
Artillery Grounds and Bunhill Fields Cemetery. Bunhill
Row itself lies parallel to the City Road, connecting
Old Street on the north with Chiswell Street on the
south; Chiswell Street connects Beech Street with

64

Finsbury Square. Walking east on Chiswell Street and turning up Bunhill Row, one passes the site a few hundred yards on the left.

Since 1585 trained bands of Londoners had marshalled for military practice in an area near Bishopsgate. In the first half of the seventeenth century the exercise ground was moved to the area near Finsbury Square, where it is still known as the Honorable Artillery Ground. Milton's house would have looked over the wall which marked its western boundary. The Artillery Ground or Artillery Garden was sometimes called Bunhill, since it lay just below Bunhill Fields: and Milton's street, the walk into the Bunhill Fields along the wall of the Artillery Ground, was called Artillery Row.

The fame which Bunhill Fields has since acquired because of the eminent dead who lie within it was just beginning in the latter part of Milton's residence nearby. The name was probably originally Bonehill, and it is known that cartloads of human bones were brought here in 1549 from the charnel house of Old St. Paul's. Early traditions make it the site of a Saxon burial ground. An inscription, now lost, once stood near the entrance, stating that the cemetery "was inclosed with a brick wall, at the sole charge of the City of London, in the Mayoralty of Sir John Lawrence, Kt., A.D. 1665; and afterwards the gates hereof were

The Bunhill Fields area. From the Newcourt-Faithorne map of 1658. Reproduced by permission of the London Topographical Society and the Map Division, The New York Public Library, Astor, Lenox and Tilden Foundations.

The east-west street in the lower right is Chiswell; Bunhill Row runs north-south from there to the western extremity of "Bun-hill."

built and finished in the Mayoralty of Sir Thomas
Bludworth, Kt., A.D. 1666."

The cemetery is often confused with the great
plague pit in Finsbury described by Defoe, which lies
farther north. The enclosure in 1665 was intended for
the benefit of the plague victims, but actually it was
not so used. It became known as the Dissenters' burial
ground. Many of the ministers who had been ejected in
1662 and were refused burial in the City churches, as
well as dissenters of all walks of life who objected
to Church of England burial rites, were buried here, a
practice which would already have begun during Milton's
last years. Later, John Bunyan, Daniel Defoe, George
Fox, and Isaac Watts were buried in the grounds.

The cemetery was closed for burials in 1852. In
1867 an Act of Parliament decreed that it must be preserved as an open space accessible to the public at
such times as were proper. In 1949 it was taken over
by the Corporation of London and made a garden of
rest, but the most important tombs and monuments were
kept. The result of all this has been, as far as Miltonists are concerned, that there is still a quiet
green area along Artillery Walk, designated now as
Bunhill Row, if not quite opposite to where Milton's
house stood, at least a little to the north, so that
it is not difficult to visualize the street as it was
in the 1670s.

The house in Bunhill Row was not large, but
there were fireplaces in at least four of the rooms,
and as always when Milton had a choice there was a
garden space (Newcourt's map of 1658 shows each house
in the row with a garden behind it). It is supposed
by some to have survived until about 1898, but French

inclines to the view that the house which then disappeared was a later one on the same site.

It was while he was living here that the last works published in his lifetime were given to the world: the History of Britain in 1670, Paradise Regained and Samson Agonistes in 1671, Of True Religion and the second edition of his Poems in 1673, and the second edition of Paradise Lost in 1674. Here also he received many visitors, including the new literary lights Dryden and Waller. Those who came to call described him as peaceful and cheerful. He liked to sit, as Richardson describes him, "in a Grey Coarse Cloth Coat at the Door of his House, near Bun-Hill Fields Without Moor-gate, in Warm Sunny Weather to Enjoy the Fresh Air, and So, as well as in his Room, received the Visits of People of Distinguish'd Parts, as well as Quality." It was in this same house that quietly and peacefully he died, a month before his sixty-sixth birthday, in November 1674.

(Bell, The Great Plague, 211; Darbishire, 75; French, Life Records, IV: 388-89; History of Bunhill Fields, 7, 13; Illustrated London News, 215: 938-39; Parker, I: 608, II: 1127; Rawlings, 24; "A Site in Moorfields," 182-83; Smith, 16; Thornbury, II: 202-3; Wheatley, I: 302.)

St. Margaret's Church, Westminster. Reproduced by
permission of the British Tourist Authority.

CHAPTER II

THE PRINCIPAL MONUMENTS

ST. MARGARET'S CHURCH, WESTMINSTER

(ST. MARGARET'S is close to the Westminster Underground station, Circle
and District lines, and to the many
buses which converge on Westminster
Abbey and the Houses of Parliament.
The easiest approach, in view of
traffic hazardous for the pedestrian,
is to follow Bridge Street, coming
away from Westminster Bridge and the
river, up to Parliament Square but to
turn left immediately, without crossing the street, on St. Margaret Street.
The church is on the south side of Parliament Square. It is then possible to
cross almost immediately, at a zebra
crossing, which leads to the church.
Do not turn left on the street but continue along the longer side of the
church and enter by its north door.
The church is actually very close to
the eastern end of Westminster Abbey,
but the usual entrance to the Abbey is
by the west door, a little farther on.)

The visitor who today steps inside the CHURCH OF
ST. MARGARET, Westminster, (and many do step into it
unknowingly, mistaking it for Westminster Abbey) en-
ters a place filled with memories of Milton, and of
the greatest interest on other scores as well. Situated on the south side of Parliament Square and opposite Westminster Hall, it was originally the transept
of the Abbey Church. It was rebuilt under Edward IV.
At the time of Edward VI the Protector Somerset, it is
said, intended to pull it down for the erection of
Somerset House; his fall saved the church from that
fate. The parish grew considerably in the first part

of the seventeenth century: between 1631 and 1638 almost 200 houses were erected in the area, usually for
people connected with the Court and their hangers-on.

St. Margaret's was Milton's parish during the
whole time of his service with the government. There
is a connection even before that time, for Areopagitica (1644) was written partly in response to a sermon
preached before the Commons in St. Margaret's demand-
ing that one of Milton's divorce tracts be censored.
The second edition of his Doctrine and Discipline of
Divorce had been dedicated to "the Parliament of England with the Assembly." On 13 August 1644 the Reverend Herbert Palmer expressed his indignation from the
pulpit of St. Margaret's: "If any plead Conscience for
the Lawfulnesse of Polygamy; (or for divorce for
other causes than Christ and His Apostles mention; Of
which a wicked booke is abroad and uncensured, though
deserving to be burnt, whose Author hath been so impu-
dent as to set his Name to it, and dedicate it to
yourselves,) or for Liberty to marry incestuously,
will you grant a Toleration for all this?" That, as
Milton was to charge, the Reverend Mr. Palmer can
scarcely have read the book, is obvious from the references to polygamy and incest.

All the records relating to Milton's short married
life with Katherine Woodcock are here. The parish
register records the marriage of "John Milton of this
Parish Esq. and Mrs. Katherin Woodcocke of the parish
of Aldermanbury Spinster" on 12 November 1656. It is
possible that the wedding took place here but more
likely that Milton availed himself of the freedom to
have a civil rather than a religious ceremony and that
the event took place at the Guildhall; we know that it
was performed by Sir John Dethicke, one of the justices

70

of the peace for London. A year later the birth of a daughter is recorded: "Katherin Milton d of John, and Katherin" with the notation beneath "This is Milton Oliver's secretary." Only a few months later the Register records the burial of both Katherines, the mother on 10 February 1658 and the baby on 20 March. The burials are recorded in a tablet in the church, but like the other graves in the former churchyard they are unidentifiable now beneath the smooth green of the lawn.

Aside from its personal associations, Milton would have been interested in the status of St. Margaret's as the official church of the House of Commons, and he may have been present at some of its historic moments. Back in 1614 James I had expressed the hope that the new Parliament would be a Parliament of Love. The phrase was taken up by some Puritan members, who proposed a corporate Communion at Westminster Abbey on Palm Sunday. On second thought, however, they decided that the services at the Abbey were too old-fashioned for their liking; so "from fear of copes and wafer-cakes" the location was changed to St. Margaret's. From that day on, 17 April 1614, St. Margaret's has been the official church of the House of Commons. Under Charles I all the Fast Day sermons were preached here, with Pym, Cromwell, Harrison, and all the other members listening from their pews. Later, after the Civil War had begun, Pym was worshipping here when word was brought to him of Edmund Waller's plot to hand the City over to the King.

It was in St. Margaret's, on 25 September 1642, that the members of both Houses, the Assembly of Divines, and the Scottish Commissioners took the Solemn League and Covenant.

71

All these historical events would have been of interest to Milton. One hopes that he would have been less interested in some of the other associations of the 1640s: the tearing down of the screen and organ loft and the mutilation of many of the tombs; or the fining of the churchwardens who in 1647 permitted a minister to preach on Christmas Day and to adorn the church with rosemary and bays. And certainly he would have regretted the treatment, after the Restoration, of the bodies of Cromwell's mother and daughter, of Pym, and of twenty others which were now disinterred and flung into a pit in St. Margaret's churchyard.

Even after the regular state services were abolished in 1859, St. Margaret's retained its status. It was here that the House of Commons gathered to give thanks for the ending of the Crimean War in 1856, of World War I in 1918, and of World War II in 1945; and the Speaker of the House still has his pew reserved.

One of the outstanding features of the present St. Margaret's is the great window dedicated to Milton in the northwestern part of the church. This tribute was inaugurated by a British clergyman and an American philanthropist.

The Dean of St. Margaret's in the latter part of the nineteenth century was the Reverend Frederic Farrar (1831-1903), noted as a writer and an educator. He improved the building both aesthetically and historically by doing away with additions made in the eighteenth century and zealously promoting the honor of the mighty dead buried within its walls. He was an admirer of the United States and had many American friends. An article by him entitled "America's Share in Westminster Abbey" appeared in the December 1887 issue of _Harper's_, where he paid tribute, among others, to "my honored friend Mr. George W. Childs, of Philadelphia," who had donated windows in Westminster Abbey in memory of George Herbert and William Cowper. At the end of the article Farrar inserted a plea for his own church. "There are," he says, "perhaps fewer memorials of Milton than of any Englishman of the same transcendent greatness. I am extremely desirous to erect a worthy window in his honor in the Church of St. Margaret's close beside the Abbey."

At about the same time Farrar wrote in the same vein to his "honored friend" George W. Childs, a successful publisher and philanthropist. Childs agreed to defray the entire cost of the memorial. Farrar expressed his gratitude and his sense of the appropriateness of the gift:

> America is the glorious child of Puritanism; and it is to me a most touching and significant fact that a memorial to Milton in the Church of the House of Commons for which he so greatly labored should now be given by a descendant of the Pilgrim Fathers. . . .

Farrar himself was to compose the inscription below the window, but he wanted a poetic tribute also. For this he asked Childs to approach John Greenleaf Whittier, whom he had called on during a visit to America in 1885 and whom he greatly admired. Whittier in turn had long admired Milton: in 1866 he had said, in a letter to his publisher: "Milton's prose has long been my favorite reading. My whole life has felt the influence of his writings."

Whittier responded by sending the lines he had composed:

> The new world honors him whose lofty plea
> For England's freedom made her own more sure,
> Whose song, immortal as its theme, shall be
> Their common freehold while both worlds endure.

In the accompanying letter he wrote:

> "I am glad to comply with thy request and
> that of our friend Archdeacon Farrar. I
> hope the lines may be satisfactory. It
> is difficult to put all that could be said
> of Milton into four lines. . . I think
> even such a scholar as Dr. Farrar will not
> object to my use of the world 'freehold.'
> Milton himself uses it in the same way
> in his prose writings, viz.: 'I too have
> my chapter and freehold of rejoicing."

The passage to which Whittier was referring occurs in the introduction to Book II of the Reason of Church Government, where Milton eloquently explains the moral compulsion to work for the good of the church: if the cause fails, he can at least console himself with the knowledge that he has done all that he could, while if the church "lift up her drooping head and prosper, among those that have something more than wished her welfare, I have my charter and freehold of rejoicing to me and my heirs."

Farrar answered that the lines were all he could desire. He remarked:

> ... they will add to the interest which all
> Englishmen and Americans will feel in the
> beautiful Milton window. I think that if

Milton had now been living, you are the
poet whom he would have chosen to speak
of him, as being the poet with whose whole
tone of mind he would have been most in
sympathy ... Unless you wish "heirloom"
to be substituted for "freehold," I will
retain the latter as the original.

The window was unveiled on Saturday, 18 February
1888. The audience at the ceremony included Robert
Browning, Lewis Morris, W. E. H. Lecky, the American
Minister Phelps, and other dignitaries. Matthew
Arnold delivered the main address, a tribute to Milton
as the supreme example in English literature of the
ideal of perfection. (The address was later printed in
Arnold's _Essays in Criticism_, Second Series.)

The window itself is designed in four panels with
three vertical sections in each, the two central sections being combined to show Milton in the act of dictating to his daughters. The other sections depict
scenes from Milton's life or from his works. These
are arranged as follows, considering the panels in
their order from left to right as one looks at them,
beginning at the top.

1. The Annunciation, with a quotation from
   PR I.134: "I sent thee to the Virgin
   pure."
2. The Nativity, with the quotation "For
   in the Inn was left no better Room."
   (PR I.248, with words slightly changed)
3. The Baptism, with the quotation "And
   he himself among them was baptized."
   (PR I.76. with words slightly changed)

4. Christ overcoming Satan: "The Tempter foiled in all his wiles." (PR I.5-6)
5. Adam and Eve in the Garden: "The Fruit of that Forbidden Tree." (PL 1.1-2)
6-7. The combined central panels showing Milton dictating.
8. Adam and Eve leaving Paradise: "Through Eden took their solitary way." (PL XII.649)
9. Satan summoning his legions: "The hollow Deep of Hell resounded." (PL 1.314-315)
10. The young Milton at St. Paul's School.
11. Milton with Galileo.
12. Adam and Eve praying: "Their vocal worship to the Choir." (PL IX.198)

Beneath the second panel is the inscription composed by Farrar: "To the glory of God and in memory of the immortal poet John Milton, whose wife and child lie buried here, this window is dedicated by George W. Childs of Philadelphia." Beneath the third panel are the lines composed by Whittier.

St. Margaret's was spared extensive injury during the bombing of World War II, but the Milton window suffered some damage; it was restored as soon as possible and was re-dedicated in a ceremony held in the church on 4 July 1949.

This time the scholar chosen to deliver the main address was Dr. E. M. W. Tillyard, Master of Jesus College, Cambridge, who under the title "Arnold on Milton" gracefully and cogently reviewed the important cultural and critical changes which had occurred since 1888 and their impact on modern attitudes toward Milton. He spoke also of the ties between Great

Britain and the United States, stronger than they had been sixty years previously, symbolized by the restoration of the window. (Tillyard's address was later printed in his Studies in Milton.)

In another part of the ceremony T. S. Eliot read Milton's sonnet beginning "Methought I saw my late espoused Saint," traditionally thought to refer to Milton's second wife, Katherine Woodcock, who, as has been seen, was buried in St. Margaret's churchyard.

(Note: The date of the unveiling ceremony in 1888 was 18 February. Almost all modern authors wrongly give it as 13 February. This probably stems from an error apparently made by Arnold himself: in a letter dated 12 February, he says he will deliver the address at the ceremony "to-morrow." But the ceremony took place on a Saturday, and the thirteenth was a Monday; all the newspaper accounts give the date as the eighteenth; and in his letter to Childs of that date Farrar says: "I have just returned from the unveiling of the Milton Window.")

(Arnold, Essays in Criticism, 34-40, Letters, II: 437; Burke, 250, 651; Childs, Recollections, 287-97; DAB, "Farrar"; Edwards, 10, 14; Farrar, Frederic, 298, 309; Farrar, Reginald, 228; French, 4, 181; Harland-Oxley, 124, 164; Jenkinson, 72-76; Kent (1951), 146; "The Milton Window," Critic 12: 94-95; Parker, I: 480, II: 1053; Pickard, II: 506, 713, 728-30; Smyth, Church and Parish, 59, 168, 204, 256, "The Commons' Church," 268; Tillyard, 1-7; Westlake, 39, 102-104; Wheatley, II: 469.)

CHALFONT ST. GILES

(The village of CHALFONT ST. GILES
can be reached from London via Route
A413; it is about twenty-five miles to
the northwest. It can be reached also by
various combinations of rail and bus.

London Country Bus No. 305 runs to
Chalfont St. Giles from either <u>Gerrard's
Cross</u> or <u>Uxbridge</u>. (It does not oper-
ate on Sundays.) No. 353 runs to the
village from <u>Amersham</u>.

<u>Gerrard's Cross</u> may be reached by
British Rail from Marylebone. <u>Uxbridge</u>
may be reached by Underground (Piccadilly
line) or by Bus No. 207. <u>Amersham</u> may
be reached by Underground (Metropolitan
line) or by British Rail from Marylebone.

Milton's cottage is on the main road of
the village, Dean Way. Get off at the
village center (near the Crown Inn) and
walk a short distance up a slight hill.
The cottage is on the left. It is
closed on Mondays and during the months
of December and January. In February
and March it is open on Saturday and
Sunday. During the rest of the year it
is open daily, except on Monday and on
Sunday morning, from 10:00 to 1:00 and
from 2:15 to 6:00.)

At the height of the great plague in the summer
of 1665 Milton took temporary refuge in a house in
CHALFONT ST. GILES.

The first cases of the epidemic had occurred in
the parish of St. Giles in the Fields. Despite the
actions of the City and the Privy Council, who in May
issued orders to close all infected houses, by June
neighboring parishes were infected, and in July the
number of deaths from plague skyrocketed: 725 in the
first week of the month, 1,089 in the second, 1,843 in
the third, and 2,010 in the fourth.

78

Part of the garden at Milton's Cottage, Chalfont St.
Giles. Reproduced by permission of the British Tourist Authority.

The area worst affected was that of Milton's parish, St. Giles Cripplegate. This was partly, no doubt, because of its location between an open ditch, two hundred feet wide and filled with sewage, on one side, and the City lay-stall in Moorfields on the other. Much of the area had originally been marshland, by this time pretty well drained and filled in; but the land remained pitted with depressions and shallow ditches where water sometimes lay stagnant.

The entries of burials in the registers of St. Giles for July fill 71 pages; 101 in August. On 18 August, 151 parishioners were buried in a single day. St. Giles coped as best it could: it purchased coffins to be used again and again for the transfer of the corpses from house to grave. The churchyard was raised two feet by the enormous number of burials. Soon many of the affected parishes had to abandon their churchyards and inter the victims in the plague pits which had been set aside, some of them not far from St. Giles itself. The last week of August saw 600 deaths in the parish which in normal times listed only 776 for a whole year.

In an effort to prevent the plague from spreading to other cities, a law was passed in the second week of June that anyone who wanted to leave London had to obtain a certificate of health; many of the villages especially in Essex and Hertfordshire resented new arrivals, some of whom developed symptoms only after arrival. Their fear is understandable, but so is the desperate desire of all who could to leave the infected city. It is estimated that two-thirds of the population of London did leave. The King and his entourage left during the first part of the summer; Parliament was prorogued first to June and then to October, when it was to meet at Oxford; the Admiralty moved to Winchester and the Exchequer to Nonesuch Palace, near Epsom. The Royal Exchange closed for two months.

It is against this background that Milton's departure for Chalfont St. Giles can be seen. In June Thomas Ellwood had happened to visit him, and Milton asked his help in securing a place in the country. Ellwood promptly found a suitable house and later recorded the event in his autobiography: "Some little time before. . . I was desired by my quondam Master Milton to take an House for him, in the Neighbourhood where I dwelt, that he might get out of the City, for the Safety of himself and his Family, the Pestilence then growing hot in London. I took a pretty Box for him in Giles-Chalfont, a Mile from me." The move probably took place shortly after the first of July.

Through wills and other documents the history of this house can be traced back to the period of Milton's occupancy. In the middle of the seventeenth century it was part of the property of George Fleetwood, who owned the Manor of Chalfont St. Giles which was known as the Vache. Fleetwood was a prominent Parliamentarian, a member of Cromwell's Council of State, who at the Restoration found himself exiled and his lands confiscated. His son John, however, retained possession of Milton's cottage, which later passed to his sister Anne. Through a succession of owners and occupants it finally passed to a Mrs. Thompson, who in 1887 sold it to the Milton's Cottage Trust.

The house still stands today a short distance from the village center, on a hill leading up to an open area. It is set close to the street; it can be entered either from the street or from a door on the

farther side through a lovely garden. Built probably
in the latter part of the sixteenth century of wattles
and daub, it was later bricked in. With a gable roof,
an exterior chimney, and lattice diamond-paned windows,
it is a charming example of an English cottage. The
house is much as it was in Milton's day, the exception
being the fact that a hallway has been added between
the present kitchen and study. A large two-storied
porch which used to stand on the garden side and
which was pulled down between 1825 and 1830 was probably added after Milton's stay.

The two rooms on the ground floor, including the
fireplaces, are just as they were, and they have been
furnished with period pieces. Since 1887 they have
also served as a museum administered by the Milton
Cottage Trust; it contains many old prints, editions
of Milton's works, copies of paintings and portraits,
facsimiles of manuscripts.

It was in this cottage that Milton lent his friend
Ellwood the manuscript of Paradise Lost, which he had
completed either shortly before he left London or
after his arrival, and here that he may have begun the
writing of Paradise Regained.

In addition to Ellwood and his Quaker friends,
there may have been others who called on Milton during
his stay there. An important family in the neighborhood was that of Isaac Penington, of nearby Chalfont
St. Peter, whose house had been visited by George Fox
in 1658; there is a tradition that Gulielma Springett,
Isaac's stepdaughter, used to come over from the
Grange to sing to Milton and play upon her lute.
Gulielma was to be the first wife of William Penn, who
after his foundation of the new colony of Pennsylvania

returned to England and eventually was buried with his two wives, children, and grandchildren at nearby Jordans, where his grave may still be seen.

By February or March of the following year the plague had abated in London enough to make it safe to return, so Milton left the village at about that time.

The setting up of the Milton Cottage Trust in 1887 is said to have been stimulated by the intention of an American to purchase it and remove it to his own country. Actually, 1887 being the year of Queen Victoria's Golden Jubilee, a Jubilee Fund was raised for the purpose, Queen Victoria heading the list of donors with a gift of twenty pounds. Ninety years later another Queen showed interest in the Cottage and another Jubilee was celebrated. Funds for the renovations and repairs necessary for the preservation of the Cottage were raised and extensive repairs undertaken during 1977. In April of that year the Queen Mother visited the Cottage, and on 27 July 1978 the Duke of Gloucester came to unveil a plaque the wording of which had been composed by Queen Elizabeth: "The restoration of this Cottage was carried out to commemorate the Silver Jubilee of Her Majesty The Queen -- A.D. 1977."

The impetus for this work of preservation and a substantial part of the funding came from an American organization founded in 1977 by Professor Ronald G. Shafer, of Indiana University of Pennsylvania, known as "The Friends of Milton's Cottage." The "Friends" remain very active in making possible the continued existence and upkeep of this very important and interesting monument.

As T. S. Eliot says, history has many cunning passages and often gives when our attention is distracted. Had not the plague in 1665-1666 sent Milton out of London, the twentieth-century visitor would not be able to enter any house where he actually lived and wrote.

(Barker and Jackson, 141; Bell, Great Plague, 48-49, 118, 146-48, 281-83; Daniell, 71; Denton, 126, 132-33; Edmonds, 21; Holmes, 117; Milton's Cottage, 5-8; Mitton, Buckinghamshire and Berkshire, 89-90; Newsletter, Friends of Milton's Cottage, June 1977, April 1978; Page, History of Buckinghamshire, III: 185-86; Parker, I: 596-98; Priestley, 79, 83-87, 95, 107-8, 115-16, 119, 149.)

ST. GILES CRIPPLEGATE

(The CHURCH OF ST. GILES CRIPPLEGATE is very close to the Aldersgate Street area as well as to Bunhill Row, but the mazes of the Barbican development can make the approach to it puzzling. It is situated in the middle of a paved terrace a little north of London Wall (the street of that name), at the corner of Wood Street and Fore Street. The simplest approach is to walk up Wood Street, from Cheapside, past the tower which is all that remains of the church of St. Alban, and to turn left through a small gate at the end of the street. Or, to avoid traffic, take the walkway just past St. Alban's on the right, at the corner of Wood Street and Addle Street. The walkway is marked Bassishaw High Walk. When the Walkway has crossed London Wall, turn left, then right, through a covered arcade, and then down the first stairway at the left. The church is open from 9:30 to 2:00 weekdays and on Saturday afternoon.)

The CHURCH OF ST. GILES WITHOUT CRIPPLEGATE was situated, as the name indicates, close to one of the main gateways in London Wall. Originally erected by the Romans, the Wall was a sign of the law and order which they established; it remained as a feature of

The Church of St. Giles, Cripplegate, as it was in the
eighteenth century. Reproduced by permission of the
Guildhall Library, City of London.

the city through medieval and early modern times. By
the sixteenth century the gates were considered police
barriers rather than military defenses. They were
still closed, according to ancient rule, when curfew
sounded from the bell of St. Martin le Grand. When the
bells of St. Nicholas Acon rang for Prime at six in
the morning, the wickets would be opened, and the gates
themselves at sunrise.

When General Monk entered the City in 1660, he removed the posts and chains in the streets, unhinged
the gates, and wedged the portcullises, thus rendering
it defenseless. Soon the gates were considered just
an obstruction, or a source of material for other struc-
tures. By an Act of Parliament of 1760 all of them
were removed.

Cripplegate was designed for pedestrians rather
than for heavier traffic. The name comes, not from
the fact that cripples begged there, although they may
have done so, but from the Old English word _crepel_,
burrow. When the Saxons conquered London in the fifth
or sixth century, they strengthened the Roman wall and
built a new gate on the northern side; from this gate
to the bastions they built a tunnel, or crepel, along
which the sentries crept to take up their positions in
the bastions.

Cripplegate was repaired and beautified many
times in its history. There were apartments over the
gateway, usually occupied by some City official, and
the gate itself had a strong apartment used as a jail
for petty offenders. It was through Cripplegate that
Elizabeth I had entered the City on 28 November 1558,
on her way from Hatfield. The site of the gate is
marked today by a plaque on Roman House.

The church of St. Giles without Cripplegate was
founded in 1090 by Alfune, thought to be a friend of
Rahere, who founded St. Bartholomew's nearby. A second
building was erected at the end of the fourteenth century, but the interior was destroyed by fire in 1545.
The church was rebuilt immediately. In 1629 the
steeple was repaired, the four corner spires taken
down and new ones of timber-work covered with lead substituted, each bearing a cross surmounted by a vane.
In 1662 a wall was erected around the churchyard, and
the burial ground was enlarged by a piece of ground
purchased from the city for 120 pounds.

The dedication of the church to St. Giles may
have had something to do with a misapprehension regard-
ing the derivation of the name Cripplegate, but not
necessarily, since the dedication was common: there
were 146 churches of the name in England. St. Giles
was a hermit of the seventh or eighth century suppos-
edly born at Athens but a resident of the south of
France; he refused to be cured of an accidental lame-
ness and became the patron of cripples. As cripples
often gathered at entrances to towns to beg, churches
to him were often found near gates.

This "fair and large church," as Stow describes
it, was just outside the area devastated by the Great
Fire in 1666, but it was the first London church to
suffer in World War II. Some damage was done, and the
rectory demolished, in the raids which began on 24
August 1940, and the fire bombs in December of that
year completed the work. Only the tower and the nave
remained intact. The fire did, however, reveal traces
of a superb fourteenth-century east window, with some
of the most beautiful traceries to be seen in any
church of the period. The window had been removed

87

when the land adjacent to the church on the north and east was built on in the sixteenth and seventeenth centuries. After the War the Corporation of London acquired this land and decided to keep it open.

The church is now an integral part of the post-war Barbican project. It stands in the center of a paved terrace nine feet above the lake which surrounds it on three sides and which has been excavated to the level of the moat which used to protect the city walls. Several sections of the ancient Roman wall are visible. On the other side of the terrace is the City of London School for Girls, constructed in such a way as to harmonize with the architecture of the church. In the recess under the church tower is a slab of Purbeck marble said to have been the doorstep of the original Norman church.

Another "survival" or relic can be found many thousands of miles away: in 1925 Bishop Johnson of the Protestant Episcopal Church in the United States visited the church and was presented with a stone from it. He took it back with him and had it incorporated into the fabric of his Cathedral Church of St. Paul, Los Angeles.

St. Giles was Milton's parish from the early 1660s until his death in 1674. Moreover, since it is here that he was buried, it is of special significance, as natural a focus for visitors as Shakespeare's birthplace is in Stratford. When Emerson visited the church in 1873, he asked, "Do many persons come to look at

Interior of the Church of St. Giles. Milton's grave is near the pulpit. Photograph by David Cockroft. Reproduced by permission of Gordon Fraser Gallery Ltd.

Milton's grave?" and the reply was, "Americans, sir."

Milton was laid to rest in the chancel on 12 November 1674, in the same grave with his father, who had died in 1647. The original gravestone had to be moved about 1679, when the two steps of the communion table were being raised. A century later the chancel was shortened when the clerestory was extended (1791), so the grave is now just outside the chancel, near the pulpit. The tablet beside it reads simply:

Near this spot was buried

John Milton

Author of Paradise Lost

Born 1608, Died 1674

The facts surrounding the notorious incident of the alleged disinterment of Milton's body have been disputed from the beginning. As noted above, the grave stone had been removed; and when the extensive repairs of 1790 were begun, the church warden gave orders to find the coffin so that the exact location would be certain. The tradition, as a matter of fact, had survived accurately, through three generations of parish clerks in the same family. The coffin was found and the grave re-closed.

About ten days later there appeared a pamphlet by a Mr. Philip Neve according to which workmen returned at night and re-opened the coffin for the benefit of relic-hunters. The truth of the account was denied almost immediately, but the most recent investigator (Read, in PMLA 45) believes that the narrative was substantially true.

The incident inspired some stanzas by William Cowper entitled "On the Late Indecent Liberties Taken

with the Remains of the Great Milton," written in
August 1790:

> Me too, perchance, in future days,
>   The sculptur'd stone shall show,
> With Paphian myrtle, or with bays
>   Parnassian, on my brow.
>
> But I, before that season come,
>   Escap'd from ev'ry care,
> Shall reach my refuge in the tomb,
>   And sleep securely there.
>
> So sang in Roman tone and style
>   The youthful bard, ere long
> Ordain'd to grace his native isle
>   With her sublimest song.
>
> Who then but must conceive disdain
>   Hearing the deed unblest
> Of wretches who have dar'd profane
>   His dread sepulchral rest?
>
> Ill fare the hands that heav'd the stones
>   Where Milton's ashes lay:
> That trembled not to grasp his bones,
>   And steal his dust away!
>
> Oh! ill-requited bard! neglect
>   Thy living worth repaid,
> And blind idolatrous respect
>   As much affronts thee dead.

(Poetical Works, ed. H. S. Milford [London: Oxford
University Press, 1934], pp. 398-99).

   The appropriateness of having a fitting monument
to Milton in the church was early acknowledged, and in
1698 Toland said there probably would be one shortly.
But, perhaps because political antagonism was still

strong, nothing came of this proposal, and the memorial had to wait for another hundred years. Finally, in 1793, a bust by the celebrated sculptor John Bacon (the elder), who, at about the same time, executed the monuments of William Pitt, Earl of Chatham, in Westminster Abbey and in the Guildhall, was placed in the church as the gift of Samuel Whitbread, known both as a friend of Sheridan and the founder of the brewery which still bears his name. The bust was placed near the grave, against a pillar on the north side of the church near the chancel.

In 1862 the bust was moved to the southwest corner of the church and the bust was enclosed in a canopied shrine designed by Edmund Woodthorpe and carved under his direction. The cenotaph, of Caen stone, was twelve feet high and nearly eight feet wide at the base, which was ornamented with a serpent, an apple, and a flaming sword. It was divided into three canopied niches by pillars of colored marble, granite, and alabaster. Beneath the bust, in the central niche, was a marble tablet:

John Milton,
Author of Paradise Lost,
Born Dec. 1608,
Died Nov. 1674,
His father, John Milton, died March 1646.
They were both interred in this church,
Samuel Whitbread posuit, 1793.

(It should be noted that 1646 is the old style date for the death of Milton senior; according to the new style, it would be 1647.)

Bombing in World War II destroyed most of the canopy, but the bust remains on the wall, opposite the north door.

In the meantime another monument began a checkered history. Wheatley, writing in the Academy for 1898, speaks of a project to convert the graveyard of St. Giles into a public garden and to place a statue or other memorial there; he notes the existence of the bust inside but holds that the public needs something outside. Six years later a bronze statue was donated by John Baddeley, a former Lord Mayor. The small plot on which it stood cost 3500 pounds, of which 2000 had been contributed by parishioners and other local contributors and 500 by the Goldsmiths' Company. Some years previously a Milton admirer had pleaded for some tangible demonstrations of more than local support for the honor of Milton: "It is to the nation at large . . . that an appeal should be made, and such an appeal could not fail to arouse a strong desire to do away with the present national disgrace of neglecting to honour Milton's tomb" (A Milton Memorial, 1862). The statue project succeeded in this to some extent: a subscription list was opened in T.P.'s Weekly, and the sums donated ranged from ten pounds ten shillings to the two shillings sixpence of "a lover of the man, a hater of the politician, but a devout admirer of the poet." Other contributors included Professor Edward Dowden, Arthur Conan Doyle, and a Chief Rabbi.

The bronze statue, the work of Horace Montford, shows Milton standing, holding a large broad-brimmed hat in his left hand, his right hand touching his chest. The head was designed to resemble the 1654 bust in Christ's College, Cambridge. The pedestal was designed by E. A. Richards; it showed the expulsion from Eden on the east and a scene from Comus on the west; there was also a quotation from Paradise Lost:

"O Spirit . . . what in me is dark / Illumine, what is
low raise and support / That to the highth of this
great argument / I may assert Eternal Providence, /
And justify the ways of God to men."

The statue was unveiled on 2 November 1904 by
Lady Egerton, a descendant of the Earl of Bridgewater,
who had a town house near the church.

At the first hit from the German bombers in August 1940 the statue was blown off the pedestal; replaced, it was again hit. Further damage from later
bombing and post-war vandalism made it inadvisable to
leave it in the open. For some time it was housed in
the headquarters of the Cripplegate Institute, a char-
itable organization in the area; some photographs of
the statue show it against the background of a staircase in that building. More recently (appropriately,
on the occasion of the wedding of a scion of the Whitbread family) it was set up inside the church, near
the Bacon bust. Part of the original pedestal may
still be seen outside.

A monument of a literary nature exists in a novel
by Hardy, The Hand of Ethelberta, published in 1876.
In chapter 27 the heroine proposes a visit to Milton's
grave, and there are some interesting descriptions of
the church as it was at the time, the second half of
the nineteenth century. The carriage containing the
party of visitors "crept along the encumbered streets
towards Barbican; till turning out of that thoroughfare
into Redcross Street they beheld the bold shape of the
old tower they sought, clothed in every neutral shade,
standing clear against the sky, dusky and grim in its
upper stage, and hoary grey below, where every corner
of every stone was completely rounded off by the

waves of wind and storm."

Inside the church, Ethelberta leans against the marble slab just below the bust of Milton, produces from her pocket a small edition of Milton, and reads from Paradise Lost. She "could be fancied a priestess of him before whose image she stood."

Hardy uses the incident to contrast the peace of the church and the reverence for the grave of a poet with the materialistic surroundings, for the church is "not many yards from the central money-mill of the world," and Ethelberta reads the line from book I: "Mammon led them on; / Mammon, the least erected spirit that fell / From heaven."

Later the visitors admire the beauty of the churchyard and are attracted by the "iron-grey bastion, partly covered by ivy and Virginia creeper, which stood obtruding into the enclosure," and which one of the party recognizes as a part of the old city wall.

Earlier in the chapter, a minor character voices what is still a common misapprehension: "I always thought that Milton was buried in Poet's Corner" [sic], Those who through this misapprehension fail to visit St. Giles' are missing one of the most important places associated with Milton's memory today.

(Baddeley, 96-97; Bell, London Wall, 71-76, 84, 97, 103, Unknown London, 30-31; Brett-James, 420-21; Clarke, 2; Daniell, 55, 65-66; Denton, 22, 55, 75-77, 80-84; Hardy, 225-37; Jenkinson, 204-05; Kent (1951) 144-45, 148, 176-78; A Milton Memorial, 17, 22, 25; Parker, II: 1201; Read, 1050-54, 1068; Saint Giles Cripplegate, 2, 3; Smith, 55, 127; Stow, I: 33, 299; "Table Talk," Gentleman's Magazine, 264: 623-24; Wheatley, "Milton and London," 201; Whitaker, 1052.)

CHAPTER III

OTHER MONUMENTS

In addition to the places directly associated with
Milton's residences that have been discussed in pre-
vious chapters, there are in London other places and
objects of special interest to the Miltonist. These
are gathered in the present chapter under three head-
ings: museums, churches other than Milton's parish
churches, and miscellaneous memorials.

MUSEUMS

> (BRITISH MUSEUM or BRITISH LIBRARY:
> on Great Russell Street, near New
> Oxford Street and Tottenham Court
> Road. From Tottenham Court Road
> station on Central and Northern lines
> walk a short distance north and east;
> from Russell Square station on Picca-
> dilly line a short distance south and
> west. Bus Nos. 7, 8, 19, 22, 25 and
> 38 run east along New Oxford Street.)

In 1973 the Library Department of the British museum was transferred from the Trustees of the British
Museum to the British Library Board and thus became
part of the British Library. The latter term is therefore more accurate than the more familiar British Museum or British Museum Library.

Outstanding among the treasures in the British
Library are Milton's family Bible and the manuscript of
his Commonplace Book. In the former (Add. MS 32310)
are recorded the entries of the births and deaths in
Milton's family; all of those up to 1650 are in his
own hand, and possibly those of 1652; after that, his
blindness made it impossible for him to write himself.
The Commonplace Book (Add. MS 36354), in which Milton
made entries from the middle 1630s until his blindness,

contains citations from eighty-six different authors.

Of special interest also is Milton's signature in Christopher Arnold's Album Amicorum (Egerton MS 1324, F. 85^V). Arnold, a distinguished visitor from Germany, persuaded Milton to write in his autograph album on 19 November 1651. Since he was almost if not totally blind by that date, he had a secretary write for him (in Greek) a quotation from 2 Cor. 12:9; "My strength is made perfect in weakness." Then he signed his own name.

Not in Milton's writing but worthy of mention is the agreement with Samuel Simmons, on 27 April 1667, for the publication of Paradise Lost (Add. MS 18861).

Henry Lawes' music for the songs in Comus (Add. MS 11518) is also of interest. There are, of course, many other manuscripts, first editions, etc. directly or indirectly relevant to Milton's biography.

(Parker, I: 389, 601; II: 793, 802, 1243-44.)

(LONDON MUSEUM: Corner of London Wall and Aldersgate Street. See directions for Aldersgate Street residence in Chapter I.)

Many tourists are unaware of the treasures contained in the LONDON MUSEUM, which happens to be situated in the heart of the Milton area. The whole of the Stuart section is more or less relevant. Of special interest is a plaque of Milton and the plans of two of the floors of the house in which he was born. Other exhibits especially worth viewing include an illuminated diagram showing the growth of London from 1550 to 1660; a diagram of Jacobean London; a large model of Whitehall Palace, and one of Old London

Bridge; Wenceslas Hollar's 1647 view of London and his
Prospect of Lincoln's Inn Fields; bills of mortality
at the time of the Plague; diagrams of the Fire; and
various articles connected with the Civil War.

> (NATIONAL PORTRAIT GALLERY: Behind
> and to the east of the National Gal-
> lery, across from St. Martins in the
> Fields, Trafalgar Square.)

In the NATIONAL PORTRAIT GALLERY is the so-called
Onslow Portrait of Milton at the age of twenty-one,
generally supposed to be one of the three authentic
portraits of the poet. There are also portraits of
many of the prominent political and literary figures
whom he knew.

> (PUBLIC RECORD OFFICE: On Chancery
> Lane, north of Fleet Street. Walk
> south on Chancery Lane from Chancery
> Lane station, Central line. Bus. No.
> 171 runs north on Chancery Lane,
> south on nearby Fetter Lane.)

The PUBLIC RECORD OFFICE contains, in addition to
a good number of official documents associated with
Milton, the manuscript copy of the Christian Doctrine
(S.P. 9/61).

> (ST. BRIDE'S CHURCH: See directions
> for Milton's residence here in
> Chapter I.)

The damage inflicted on ST. BRIDE'S CHURCH by
World War II bombing had an unforeseen result. Excavations made during rebuilding operations revealed extensive traces of the medieval, Saxon, and Roman

buildings which had stood on the site, as well as various artifacts. Some of the earlier stone work can be seen in the crypt, which houses a permanent exhibition of the history of the site as well as material on the history of Fleet Street as the home of print. Of special interest are fragments of glass from the old church, charred wood from the pre-Fire level, diagrams of the area in the sixteenth, seventeenth, eighteenth, and nineteenth centuries, and records of the Plague and the Fire. There is a reproduction of a portrait of Milton and of the title page of Starkey's <u>The Dignity of Kingship Asserted: in Answer to Mr. Milton's "Ready and Easie Way to establish a free commonwealth."</u>

(Morgan, 235, 263-65.)

CHURCHES

In addition to the parish churches described in connection with his residences, there are several other churches in the City of London which have some associations with Milton. Most of the city churches, of course, have had to recover from two major disasters; the Great Fire of 1666 and the bombing of 1940-45. Statistics tell part of the story. Before the Fire, the City of London counted 109 parish churches; of these eighty-seven were totally destroyed and others damaged. Of those which had been destroyed, Wren rebuilt forty-nine. Almost without exception these were built on the old foundations, sometimes even as copies of those destroyed;that fact preserves for them some of their aura of antiquity.

Although some of the old churches and some of the

rebuilt ones had succumbed to decay in the eighteenth
and nineteenth centuries, there were still forty-seven
churches within the City boundaries before the outbreak
of World War II. Of this number twenty were completely
destroyed or damaged beyond repair.

Some of those connected with Milton were involved
in both disasters, but in many cases it is possible to
identify features which form real links with the past.
(Cobb, 2; Daniell, 3; Mead, 301-302; Reddaway, 298;
Trent, 264.)

(ST. ANNE BLACKFRIARS and ST. ANDREW
IN THE WARDROBE: The present St.
Andrew's, and the site of St. Anne's,
are on the north side of the western
part of Queen Victoria Street, just
east of New Bridge Street and close to
the Blackfriars Underground station,
Circle and District Lines. Bus No. 76
operates on Queen Victoria Street.
Buses for St. Paul's are also convenient
for the western part of Queen Victoria
Street.)

Milton's friend Charles Diodati was buried in St.
Anne's on 27 August 1638. Milton was in Italy at the
time, and it seems likely that the ties of friendship
must have brought him on his return to visit Diodati's
grave, fulfilling the promise made poetically in the
Latin elegy, "Epitaphium Damonis"; "Whatever befalls,
Damon, you may be sure...that you shall not turn to
dust in the sepulcher unmourned."

Originally part of the Priory of the Black Friars,
the parish church, which was already distinct from the
friars' church, was rebuilt in 1613. It was destroyed
in the Fire, and the parish was united with that of
ST. ANDREW IN THE WARDROBE. Two churchyards of St.

101

Anne's survive, both close to the present church of St.
Andrew: one in Church Entry and one in Ireland Yard,
both now maintained as gardens by the City Corporation
for St. Andrew's. The Ireland Yard garden contains
the only remaining fragment of the original Priory, as
well as a stone stating the boundaries of St. Anne's
parish. Shakespeare and Jonson both had houses nearby,
and Ireland Yard is the probable site of a house on
which Shakespeare took a mortgage, the deed for which,
with his signature, is in the British Library.

(Bulmer-Thomas, 11; French, Life Records, I: 371;
Jenkinson, 23334.)

(ST. CLEMENT DANE'S: The church is
situated on an "island" in the Strand,
at the eastern end of Aldwych. It is
accessible from the Temple Underground
station, Circle and District lines;
walk north on Arundel or Surrey Street
and turn east on the Strand. Bus Nos.
in the Strand include 6, 11, 15, and
77.)

Two of Milton's nephews, sons of his brother,
Christopher, were baptized in ST. CLEMENT DANE'S:
John on 29 June 1643 and Thomas on 2 February 1647. It
was in St. Clement's Churchyard that Mary Powell lived
with Christopher's mother-in-law for a short time, in
the interval after the dramatic reconciliation in the
house in St. Martin's le Grand.

The name of the church came from the fact that
King Harold, of the Danish line, as well as other Danes,
were buried there. In the early days it was in the possession of the Knights Templars. Eventually Elizabeth
I bestowed it on Lord Burleigh. At the time of the
Essex rebellion a gun was placed on top of the tower,
commanding Essex House. John Donne's wife, Anne, was

buried here and is commemorated by a plaque. In 1640 the church was rebuilt in the classical style. It was severely damaged by fire in 1941 but has been restored. The crypt, now the Royal Air Force Chapel, is old.

(French, Life Records, II: 177; Jenkinson, 245-46; Jesse, I: 342; Parker, I: 234.)

(ST. GEORGE THE MARTYR is in Borough High Street, Southwark, the road that leads directly south from London Bridge; it is about half a mile from the river, at the intersection of the High Street with Great Dover Street and Long Lane and is directly opposite the Borough Underground station, Northern line. Bus Nos. 10, 21, 35, 40, 95 and 133 pass it.)

An event of 1656 may have brought Milton to this church: on the death of Cromwell, "his body was brought in the morning to St. George's Church in Southwark, at which place at 12 of the clock his friends and many of the clergy and gentry met and accompanied it thence to Somerset House."

The church was in good condition at the time, having been repaired and decorated in 1629 and again in 1652, but it was rebuilt entirely in the eighteenth century.

For some undiscovered reason, the church was one of two choices for the marriage to Elizabeth Minshull: the application for the marriage license, signed by Milton, asks permission to be married either in the church of St. George in Southwark or in that of St. Mary Aldermary in London. The wedding actually took place in the latter. Neither was the parish church of the bride.

(French, <u>Life Records</u>, IV: 381; Jenkinson, **267-68**; <u>Survey of London</u>, 25:27.)

> (ST. MARTIN-IN-THE-FIELDS, on the
> northeast side of Trafalgar Square,
> just opposite the National Portrait
> Gallery, is close to the Charing
> Cross station on Bakerloo, Northern
> and Jubilee lines as well as to many
> bus routes.)

The family of Milton's sister Anne, who in 1623
had married Edward Phillips, lived in the parish of
ST. MARTIN-IN-THE-FIELDS. The baptismal and death
registers tell a story of infant mortality only too
common in the seventeenth century: their daughter
Anne was baptized in 1626, buried in 1628; Elizabeth
was baptized 1628, buried 1631; John was baptized 1625,
buried 1629. The first child, Anne, was the subject
of Milton's early poem "To a Fair Infant Dying of a
Cough." A little later (August 1631) Edward Phillips
himself died, and Anne was left a widow.

Milton was in Cambridge for most of these years
but may have been home for some of the baptisms or
funerals. Evidence that has recently come to light
shows the possibility of a closer connection. In May
of 1627 John Milton the elder bought a house in the
area, and there is a possibility that the Milton family lived here for a while before moving to Hammersmith.

The church itself had an interesting origin. At
the time of Henry VIII the inhabitants of St. Martin's
Fields had no parish church but used the church of St.
Margaret in Westminster, "and thereby were forced to
carry their dead bodies by the Court Gate of Whitehall,
which the said King Henry then misliking, caused the

104

Church in the Parish of St. Martins in the Fields to
be erected and made a Parish there." The building was
late Gothic in style, with a tower surmounted by a
bell turret. The roof of the nave had dormer windows,
and there was a sundial on the wall over the west window. Under the Commonwealth it was selected as a
place for public penance. It was entirely rebuilt in
the eighteenth century.

(Brett-James, 110; Clavering and Shawcross, 685;
French, Life Records, I: 89, 103, 152, 153, 190, 227,
243; Jenkinson, 253-55.)

> (The site of the church of ST. MARY
> ALDERMANBURY, marked now by a garden,
> was at the corner of Love Lane and
> Aldermanbury Street, south of Basing-
> hall, just northwest of the Guildhall.
> St. Paul's (Central), Bank (Central),
> and Moorgate (Northern) are within
> walking distance. Approaching from
> London Wall on the north, Bus No. 141
> is convenient; from Cheapside on the
> south, 8, 22, 25 or 501.)

ST. MARY ALDERMANBURY was the parish of Katherine
Woodcock, Milton's second wife, and it is possible
that the marriage in 1656 took place in this church
(not to be confused with St. Mary Aldermary), but it
is more probable that the place was the Guildhall. The
marriage took place under the Protectorate, and Milton
would have been free to follow his conviction that
marriage is a civil contract, not a sacrament. The
church register, however, records the event: "The
agreement and intention of marriage between John
Milton, Esq., of the parish of Margaret's in Westminster
and Mrs. Katherine Woodcocke of Mary's in Aldermanbury,
was published three several market days in three
several weeks,...and no exception being made against

their intentions, they were, according to the Act of
Parliament, married on the 12th of November, by Sir
John Dethicke, Knight and Alderman, one of the Jus-
tices of the Peace for the City of London."

John Heminge and Henry Condell, the editors of
Shakespeare's First Folio, lived in the parish and
were buried here; Shakespeare himself attended it when
he was in London. Edmund Calamy, a distinguished Puritan opponent of episcopacy, was the incumbent from
1639 to 1662.

Rebuilt after the Fire, then badly damaged by
bombing, the church has the unique distinction of having been re-erected in the United States, at Westminster College, Fulton, Missouri, as a memorial to
Winston Churchill, who made his famous Iron Curtain
speech here on 5 March 1946. The College established
the Churchill Memorial and Library to commemorate the
event and the man; it arranged to transfer and rebuild
the ruined church of St. Mary Aldermanbury as a symbol
of faith in man's will to endure as well as the friendship between England and America. The foundation
stone was laid by the Bishop of London in October 1966,
and the restoration was carefully carried out.

The church has left behind on the site one of the
loveliest small gardens in London. Some foundations
from the ancient church surround the area, which en-
shrines a bust of Shakespeare erected as a memorial to
Heminge and Condell.

(Garwood, 182; Jenkinson, 173; Trent, 264; Wheatley,
II: 490-91; Winston Churchill Memorial, 1-3.)

> (The church of ST. MARY ALDERMARY
> is at the corner of Watling Street
> and Queen Victoria Street, near the
> Mansion House and the Mansion House
> station, Circle and District Lines.
> Bus No. 76 traverses Queen Victoria
> Street.)

Milton was married to his third wife, Elizabeth Minshull, in the Church of ST. MARY ALDERMARY, which still stands, though much altered, at the corner of Watling Street and Queen Victoria Street. The present church is Wren's but much of the pre-Fire church was incorporated into the new fabric, which is thought to stand entirely on its old foundations. The traceried heads of the windows in the south aisle are pre-Fire, and the arches are on the same lines as the old church, though the work on them is later.

(French, Life Records, IV: 386; A Short History of the Church of St. Mary Aldermary, 1-2; Smyth, Church and Parish, 64-65.)

OTHER MEMORIALS

> (MILTON STREET is close to the Moor-
> gate station, Northern, Circle, and
> Metropolitan lines. Walk north on
> Moorgate, turn left at Ropemaker
> Street, which leads into Milton Court
> and thence to Milton Street. The most
> convenient buses are those on City
> Road, which is a continuation of Moor-
> gate; Nos. 76, 104, 141, 214, and 271.)

There are various memorials to Milton scattered throughout London. Among these may be included the name of MILTON STREET. Authorities have differed on whether or not it was named for the poet: Denton, Ekwall, Harben and Hare maintain that the name was adopted in memory of the carpenter and builder who had speculated in buying up the leases of the old houses in the street, while Kent, Masson, Thornbury, and Smith say that it was named for the poet. Since all agree that the change was made in 1830, and since Kent quotes the 1829 petition for the change, the second position seems the correct one. The petition suggested the name "Milton Street," says the document, "to show that while the inhabitants of the greatest commercial city in the world are attentive to their own interests, they are not unmindful of the claims of Literature and Science."

What is indubitable is that the street is in the neighborhood which is most closely associated with the poet. It runs south from Chiswell Street almost exactly opposite Artillery Row. Originally, as Grub Street, it was somewhat longer; inhabited, as Johnson says, "by writers of small histories, dictionaries, and temporary poems," it became a synonym for hack writing. Masson was probably close to the mark when he said that the reason for the change of name in 1830 was partly to commemorate the fact that Milton had lived nearby but partly also to get rid of the old associations.

(Denton, 174; Ekwall, 85; Harben, 416; Hare, I: 273; Kent (1970), 278; Lang, 211; Masson, Life, VI: 485; Smith, 139; Thornbury, II: 240.)

VISUAL MONUMENTS

(WESTMINSTER ABBEY: Across the street (west) from the House of Parliament, Westminster station, Circle lines; many buses.)

(ATHENAEUM: On Pall Mall, corner of Waterloo Street; close to Trafalgar Square.)

(CITY OF LONDON SCHOOL: On the
Victoria Embankment, close to
Blackfriars Bridge and New Bridge
Street. Blackfriars station, Circle
and District lines. Bus No. 131
traverses the Embankment.)

(GUILDHALL: Near Gresham Street.
See the directions for St. Mary
Aldermanbury in the first part of
this chapter.)

Of the visual monuments in the City, the bust in
WESTMINSTER ABBEY is the best known. It was not
erected until 1737, but Milton's name had appeared in
the Abbey on an earlier occasion: the epitaph for the
statue of John Philips (not Milton's nephew, but the
poet, who died in 1709) alluded to him as "Uni Miltono
Secundus, primoque paene par." Dean Sprat had the al-
lusion erased lest the walls of the Abbey be polluted
by Milton's name, but Dean Atterbury had it recut four
years later.

A Dutch sculptor, John Michael Rysbrack, was em-
ployed by William Benson to design the monument, which
was duly placed on the wall in the Poets' Corner. It
was subsequently widely reproduced in black Wedgwood
ware. Benson, who was a critic, politician, and patron
of belles-lettres, composed the inscription:

> In the year of our Lord Christ One
> Thousand Seven Hundred and Thirty-
> Seven This Bust of the author of
> Paradise Lost was placed here by
> William Benson Esquire one of ye
> two Auditors of the Imprests to His
> Majesty King George the Second for-
> merly Surveyor General of the Works
> to His Majesty King George the first
> Rysbrack was the statuary who cut it.

109

The inscription inspired two well-known quips: Pope
wrote "On poets' tombs see Benson's titles writ," and
Johnson remarked to Boswell: "Mr. Benson has bestowed
more words upon himself than upon Milton." And someone
remarked to Johnson: "I have seen erected in that
church a bust of that man whose name I once knew considered a pollution to its walls."

The bust is in the east aisle of the south transept of the Abbey, in the southwest corner of the
aisle and therefore of the Poets' Corner proper, which
has overflowed into the western aisle of the transept
also. Visitors may not always notice that Milton is
mentioned in the inscription to Gray's monument immediately below:

> No more the Graecian Muse unrival'd reigns:
> To Britain let the Nations homage pay;
> She felt a Homer's fire in Milton's strains,
> A Pindar's rapture in the Lyre of Gray.

Of interest also is the quotation from Paradise Lost
(Book V, 898-902) elsewhere in the Abbey, on a tablet
in memory of the Earl of Oxford and Asquith:

> ...Unmoved
> Unshaken, unseduced, unterrified,
> His loyalty he kept, his love, his zeal;
> Nor number nor example with him wrought
> To swerve from truth, or change his
> constant mind.

The library of THE ATHENAEUM houses a bust which
is a copy of Rysbrack's, presented to the Club by
Trollope's widow. The inscription reads:

Presented
by
Mrs. Trollope
to the
Athenaeum
by desire of her late Husband
Anthony Trollope
A Member
--1883--

In company with Bacon, Shakespeare, and Newton, Milton stands high on the facade of the CITY OF LONDON SCHOOL, opposite the Victoria Embankment near Blackfriars. In the window in the old library of the GUILDHALL his figure is shown on the bottom right, next to Stow and directly below Coverdale.

We may close this section with a description of a memorial which had a brief existence of seventy-five years at the corner of Park Lane and Hamilton Place but was demolished in 1949 in the interests of traffic. This was a memorial fountain inscribed "To the Fathers of English Poetry." On a pedestal were the figures of Chaucer (looking down Hamilton Place), Shakespeare (up Park Lane), and Milton (across the park). On the apex was Fame blowing her trumpet. The monument was the work of Thomas Thornycroft. It does not seem to have been much lamented, but one wishes that London would erect some other memorial to one of its greatest sons.

(Esdaile, English Church Monuments, 114-15; Frederic Farrar, 309, 150; Kent (1951), 144, 148-49; Parker, II: 1200-01.)

LEX IGNEA:
OR
The School of Righteousnes.

A
SERMON
Preach'd before the KING,
Octob. 10. 1666.

At the SOLEMN FAST appointed
For the late
FIRE in LONDON.

By WILLIAM SANCROFT. D.D.
Dean of S. Pauls.

Published by His Majesties special Command.

Etiam periere Ruinæ

W. Hollar fecit A. 1688.

London, Printed for Timothy Garthwait. 1666.

CHAPTER IV

THE GREAT FIRE AND THE GREAT WAR

Since the Fire of 1666 and the bombing during
World War II are significant factors in the history of
London, and since the former occurred while Milton was
still living, these two events are here described
briefly from the viewpoint of their impact on Milton's
London.

THE FIRE

The Great Fire of London ravaged the city not
long after Milton had returned from Chalfont St. Giles.
News of the conflagration would doubtless have been
brought to him in his house in Jewin Street. Before
it ended, the fire would have come uncomfortably close
to his home, but probably no one suspected this on the
first day. What would have been apparent was the danger to the property he owned in Bread Street. He
could not see the flames which Pepys described as "one
entire arch of fire" but would be able to hear the
rumbling of carts as refugees streamed to Moorfields.

Some steps to prevent fires in London had been
taken as far back as 1189. In the sixteenth century
wooden chimneys were forbidden and the reredos of
every hearth had to be fireproof; a little later
James I decreed that all new houses should be built of
brick. The provision was carried out to some extent by

Old St. Paul's in flames. Engraving by Wenceslas
Hollar on the title page of a sermon preached a month
after the Great Fire of 1666. Reproduced by permission
of the Print Collection, Art, Prints and Photographs
Division, The New York Public Library, Astor, Lenox
and Tilden Foundations.

the wealthy, but the houses of the poor could be built
in a day and so could be done surreptitiously; the
wooden frame would be made in a secret place, then
taken to its site, laid on its sills, and bolted to-
gether. Methods of firefighting had been organized;
every citizen had to keep a barrel of water outside
his house during the dry months, and every ward had to
have a firehook to pull down the beams and rafters of
burning buildings. Churchwardens were required to
keep ladders, hooks, and buckets ready in the church.
In a crisis, neighbors would come and form chains link-
ing the fire with the nearest source of water. But
such measures were of little avail in a major fire.

Pudding Lane, where the fire began on 1 September
1666, runs parallel to Fish Street Hill from Eastcheap
to Lower Thames Street. Thomas Farynor, the King's
baker, lived with his family and two servants in a
house near the foot of the hill. On the night of Saturday, 1 September, he had drawn the fire as usual;
but about midnight he had to strike a fresh light,
and this apparently started the blaze. It was discov-
ered before morning, but the staircase was already cut
off; however, everyone except one maid escaped on to
the roof through an upstairs window. (The maid was
afraid of heights.)

The wind which came up ignited neighboring buildings, including the Star Inn in Fish Street Hill, in
whose yard bales of hay were stored. Soon the fire
reached St. Magnus Martyr and swept along the water-
front as far as Baynard's Castle. By evening its two
arms had joined to form a huge arc from a point east
of the Bridge along Eastcheap and Cannon Street. Meantime, the King and the Duke of York (who were and are
praised even by their enemies for their conduct during

114

the crisis) were ordering the pulling down of houses to create a gap and were working alongside the ordinary citizens.

On Monday morning fire posts were set up for men and materials, each under the command of three Justices of the Peace, with thirty infantrymen attached to each. One of these was near the Wall at Cripplegate. Throughout the day the flames kept creeping through Gracechurch, Threadneedle, and Poultry Streets. By this time so many people were streaming out of the City and there was such confusion at the gates, with people and carts leaving and other carts coming in to transport goods, that the magistrates forbade any carts to come near the fire.

By Monday night Bread Street was gone, with the churches of St. Mildred's and All Hallows. The next day more drastic measures were taken: houses were blown up on the north and east, checking the fire at the Tower and just below Cripplegate. On the west, however, the flames were victorious, sweeping down Newgate and Ludgate. St. Paul's at last caught fire; it burned all Tuesday night and all day Wednesday. The flames were finally checked at Fetter Lane.

On Wednesday night and Thursday small fires kept breaking out, one of them near Cripplegate; it burned all day Wednesday and was put out only late at night. By Thursday morning, the sixth, the fire could be said to be over. It was on that morning that the King went to Moorfields, where many of the refugees had gathered. He assured the people that the rumors about the origin of the fire -- that it had been set by the Dutch, or the French, or the Papists -- were not true; he promised he would continue to defend his subjects and asked them not to yield to alarm or suspicion.

Later the City Surveyors reported that 373 acres (five-sixths of the area) within the walls had been burned, as well as 63 acres outside; 13,200 houses in more than 400 streets and courts had gone, and 100,000 people were homeless. Besides 87 churches and 6 chapels, many public buildings had been destroyed or irreparably damaged, among them the Royal Exchange, the Guildhall, the Custom House, the Herald's Office, and a large part of the Inner Temple. Remarkably, there were very few lives lost: only eight seem to have been directly due to the flames, although the indirect number must have been greater.

In common with other scholarly Londoners, Milton must also have lamented the tremendous loss of books caused by the Fire. According to Pepys, some of the booksellers in St. Paul's Churchyard were wholly undone. The fire had consumed not only those in the churchyard itself but also those in St. Faith's (the crypt of St. Paul's) and the nearby warehouses. Several days after the Fire Pepys lamented that a great lack of books, especially Latin and foreign publications, was foreseen, and he mentions especially the scarcity of copies of Walton's six-volume polyglot Bible. Milton would no doubt be especially concerned if he learned that Samuel Cromleholme, then Master of St. Paul's School, had lost his library, which was supposed to be the best private collection in London at that time.

Plans for rebuilding were made at once, and some of the projects had reached completion before Milton's death. Wren's great plan for a city rebuilt on logical lines, with avenues radiating out from a new St. Paul's, was turned down, and London was rebuilt along its

original lines. Some frontages were set back, some
alleys leading to the Thames were levelled, and King
and Queen Streets were cut from the Guildhall to the
Thames; otherwise, the ground plan of the City was vir-
tually unaltered.

The rejection of the most drastic plans for rebuilding has been lamented and criticized ever since.
It must be realized, however, that plans for improve-
ment had to be practical: anything involving undue
delay would have to be rejected. Many citizens were
homeless; various essential trades had to go on; and
financing would have to be done largely by private en-
terprise. What the two Rebuilding Acts which were
passed soon after the Fire were able to do was to lay
down regulations for improving streets and houses: new
buildings were to be of brick or stone, and there were
regulations about size and positions.

The destruction of the Bread Street area removed
from history not only Milton's birthplace but some of
the churches and other buildings associated with him --
St. Paul's School, All Hallows Church, and others. Of
the twenty-two churches left unharmed by the Fire,
three were associated with him: St. Bartholomew the
Great, St. Botolph Aldersgate, and St. Giles Cripplegate. By the time he died thirteen of the ruined
churches had already been rebuilt.

(Barker and Jackson, 144-45; Bell, The Great Fire,52-
55, 88, 92, 108-10, 147, 166, 174-77, 334; Brett-James,
28; Masson, Life, VI: 504; Mead, 301-302; Pepys, 267-
81, 297, 309-10; Priestley, 55, 151-77; Reddaway, 48,
80.)

WORLD WAR II

The ravages of the Fire of 1666 could not compare
with the results of the five-year period of World War
II. An idea of the devastation can only be suggested
sketchily by statistics. In the first air raid of 7
September 1940, 375 bombers came over the city; and
for the next fifty-seven nights, without a break, an
average of two hundred bombers a night attacked. By
the following May, 50,000 bombs had fallen on the city.

The greatest single disaster, and the one which
most affected the area most closely connected with
Milton, was the great fire-raid of 29 December. The
entire area between St. Paul's and the Guildhall was
practically levelled, and the Church of St. Giles
Cripplegate was severely damaged.

After 1940-41, the most intensive bombing period
was in February-March of 1944 and again in June of that
year.

By the end of the war, from a total of 460 acres
of built-up land in the City, buildings covering 164
acres had been damaged. In Greater London, 10,000 of
2,200,000 dwellings were destroyed; seventy-five per-
cent received damage of some kind.

Heartbreaking as was the wholesale destruction,
it afforded the opportunity for some imaginative rebuilding, which after inevitable delays became a reality. In 1959, a new street was created, called London
Wall, running east from Aldersgate to Moorgate; around
it were erected two-hundred-foot-high office buildings.
The new London Museum is located just where the street
begins, and north of it rise the forty-three-story
towers designed to bring back 6,500 residents into the

City and to enable them to live conveniently and pleas-
antly. Many of the pavements are raised eighteen feet
above road level -- a boon to the pedestrian if he
does not get lost in the maze; there are shops and
public houses, underground car parks, and all the other
paraphernalia of a city within a city. Cultural centers, some of them already in existence, are planned
to include, besides the London Museum and the Guildhall School of Music and Drama, a library, an art gallery, and centers for the London Symphony Orchestra and
the Royal Shakespeare Theater. This entire redevelop-
ment area is called the Barbican.

(Barker and Jackson, 368; Garrett, 610, 612; Henrey,
2-18; Jones, 348; Kent (1970), 20, 40;Whitaker, 1052.)

Many of the buildings which fire and war left intact disappeared with the slow decay of time or as a
sacrifice to progress in the shape of improved mass
transit and traffic devices. Yet enough of the old
London is left to enable us to stand in places where
Milton stood, to walk along the streets which still
follow the same meandering paths, and to reconstruct
from what remains the London that was part of his ex-
perience.

APPENDIX

SUGGESTED ROUTES

For the places outside of London, someone traveling
by car might visit more than one local area on one day.
The traveler by bus or train might do some combining,
if necessary: Harefield lies near one of the routes to
Chalfont St. Giles, and Langley is only a few miles
from Horton. Forest Hill, which is near Oxford, re-
quires a day by itself, and Ludlow demands an overnight
stay.

In London itself a tourist with sufficient time
could visit the Miltonic areas in their chronological
order. Many, however, would no doubt prefer to cover
the city area by area. The following paragraphs suggest
some practical ways of proceeding.

1. Beginning with the site of Milton's birthplace
   in Bread Street, visit the nearby church of
   St. Mary le Bow before walking down Watling
   Street to St. Paul's. From St. Paul's walk
   north on Aldersgate Street (from which Jewin
   Street and Barbican once branched off), visit
   the church of St. Botolph, and follow Little
   Britain to Bartholomew Close and the church of
   St. Bartholomew. (Map 1.)

2. More or less in the same area, go first to the
   church of St. Giles Cripplegate, then up Milton
   Street to Bunhill Row. (Map 1.)

3. The site of the residence in High Holborn,
   near Lincoln's Inn Fields, forms a natural
   unit with Red Lion Square and the church of St.
   Giles in the Fields. (Map 2.)

121

4. The Charing Cross and Whitehall residences, with the church of St. Martin in the Fields, could be a starting point for a walk to St. Margaret's Church and thence to Petty France. (Map 3.)

5. A visit to St. Bride's Church, with the museum in the crypt, could be followed by a walk to St. Andrew in the Wardrobe, thence to St. Mary Aldermanbury and the site of St. Mary Aldermary. (Map 1.)

Hammersmith and the churches of St. George the Martyr and St. Clement Dane lie somewhat off the beaten track, although St. Clement's is not far from any of the routes described above.

The various museums will no doubt require separate visits of longer duration; but some time could be spent at the London Museum in connection with Route 2 and at the British Museum with Route 3.

MAPS OF MODERN LONDON

The following three maps of sections of modern
London were drawn by Karen McCann. They are based on
a map published by the British Tourist Authority. The
maps show the three principal areas that have Miltonic
associations. The principal streets and landmarks have
been indicated here, as well as the names of the
streets particularly associated with Milton.

Map 1.
The area near St. Paul's where Milton lived during
his early years and immediately after his return from
Italy. In the northeast part of the map is Bunhill
Row, where he spent his last years.

Map 2.
Holborn and the British Museum area. Near the
center of the map are Lincoln's Inn Fields, near which
Milton lived in the late 1640s, and Red Lion Square,
where he lived for a short time after coming out of
hiding in 1660.

Map 3.
Westminster. Charing Cross and Whitehall, where
Milton lived fron 1649 to 1651, were near Trafalgar
Square, in the upper right. Below St. James Park is
Petty France, his residence from 1652 to 1660.

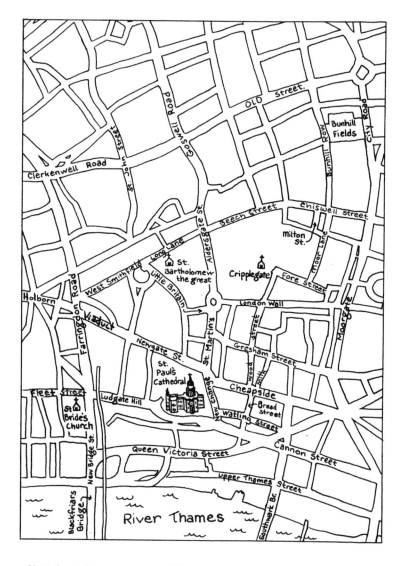

Map 1.   The area near St. Paul's.

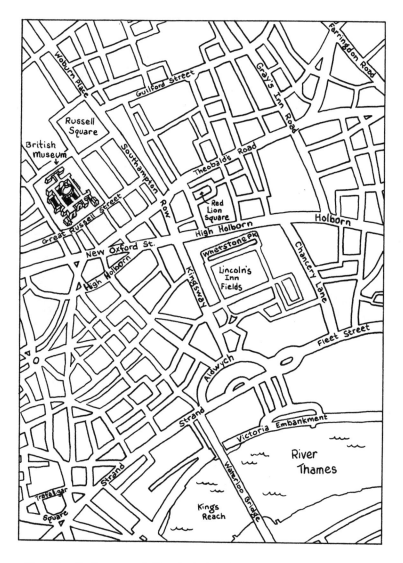

Map 2. Holborn and the British Museum area.

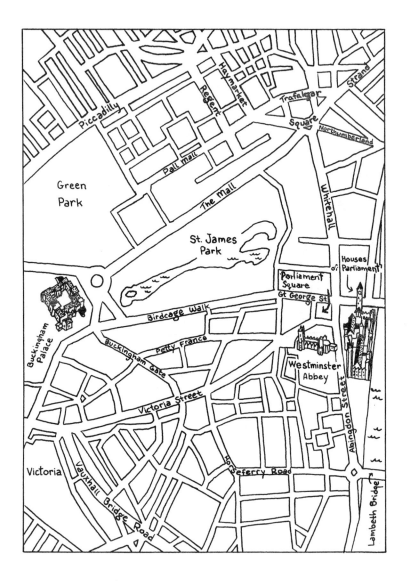

Map 3. Westminster.

BIBLIOGRAPHY

Allison, J. W. "Milton--Baptismal Font." Notes and
      Queries, 27 Oct. 1888, p. 324.

Archer, J. W. Vestiges of Old London. London:
      D. Bogue, 1851.

Arnold, Matthew. "Milton." In his Essays in Criticism.
      2d ser. London: Macmillan, 1888, pp. 34-40.

_____. Letters of Matthew Arnold. Ed. G. W. E.
      Russell. New York: Macmillan, 1896.

Athenaeum, 5 Nov. 1864, p. 603. [On the house in
      Barbican.]

Baddeley, J. J. An Account of the Church and Parish of
      St. Giles, Without Cripplegate. London: n.p.,1888.

Barker, Felix, and Jackson, Peter. London: Two Thou-
      sand Years of a City and Its People. New York:
      Macmillan, 1974.

Beeson, Trevor. "Financial Crisis at St. Margaret's."
      Christian Century 87 (1970): 956.

Bell, Walter George. The Great Fire of London in 1666.
      London: John Lane, 1920.

_____. The Great Plague in London in 1665. London:
      Bodley Head, 1924.

_____. London Wall through Eighteen Centuries. Lon-
      don: Council for Tower Hill Improvement, 1937.

_____. Unknown London. London: Spring Books, 1966.

Besant, Walter. London in the Time of the Stuarts.
      London: A. and C. Black, 1903.

Betjeman, John. The City of London Churches. London:
      Garrod and Lofthouse, 1974.

Blakiston, Noel. "Milton's Birthplace." London Topo-
      graphical Record 19 (1947): 1-12.

Boynton, Percy H. London in English Literature.
      Chicago: University of Chicago Press, 1913.

Brett-James, Norman G. The Growth of Stuart London.
      London: Allen and Unwin, 1935.

Brewer, H. W. Old London Illustrated. London: The
      Builder, 1962.

Bulmer-Thomas, Ivor. St. Andrew-by-the-Wardrobe with
      St. Ann Blackfriars. London: Published by the
      Rector and Churchwardens, 1969.

Burke, Arthur M., ed. Memorials of St. Margaret's
    Church, Westminster. London: Eyre and Spottis-
    woode, 1914.

Bush, Graham. Old London. London: Academy Editions, 1975.

Chancellor, Edwin B. The History of the Squares of
    London. London: K. Paul, 1907.

_____. The Private Palaces of London, Past and
    Present. Philadelphia: Lippincott, 1909.

Childs, George William. Recollections. Philadelphia:
    Lippincott, 1892.

Christ's College, Cambridge. Cambridge: Pendragon
    Press, n.d.

Clark, Donald L. John Milton at St. Paul's School.
    New York: Columbia University Press, 1948.

Clarke, Hervey Adams. A History of the Parish Church
    of St. Giles. Beaconsfield: n.p., 1961.

Clavering, Rose, and Shawcross, John T. "Anne Milton
    and the Milton Residences." Journal of English
    and Germanic Philology 59 (1960): 680-90.

Cobb, Gerald. The Old Churches of London. New York:
    Scribner, 1942.

Cowper, William. The Poetical Works. Ed. H. S. Mil-
    ford. 4th Ed., London: Oxford University Press,
    1934.

Daniell, Alfred E. London City Churches. Westminster:
    Constable, 1895.

Darbishire, Helen, ed. The Early Lives of Milton.
    London: Constable, 1932.

Darlington, Ida, and Howgego, James. Printed Maps of
    London, 1553-1850. London: Philip, 1964.

Demaray, John G. Milton and the Masque Tradition. Cam-
    bridge, Mass.: Harvard University Press, 1968.

Denton, William. Records of St. Giles' Cripplegate.
    London: G. Bell, 1883.

Dictionary of American Biography. Vol. 4, 1930. S.v.
    "Childs, George William."

Dictionary of National Biography. Vol. 4, 1921-22.
    S.v. "Colet, John." Vol. 2 of Second Supplement,
    1912. S.v. "Farrar, Frederic William."

Eagle, Dorothy, and Carnell, Hilary. The Oxford Liter-
    ary Guide to the British Isles. Oxford: Oxford
    University Press, 1977.

Edmonds, G. C. <u>Milton in Buckinghamshire</u>. Chalfont St. Giles: Richard Sadler, 1976.

Edwards, David L. <u>St. Margaret's, Westminster</u>. London: Garrod and Lofthouse, 1973.

Ekwall, Eilert. <u>Street-Names of the City of London</u>. Oxford: Clarendon Press, 1954.

Eldredge, H. Wentworth, ed. <u>World Capitals</u>. Garden City: Doubleday, 1975.

Esdaile, Katharine A. "A Problem and a Parallel." <u>London Times</u>, 10 Aug. 1938, p. 15.

_____. <u>English Church Monuments 1510 to 1840</u>. New York: Oxford University Press, 1946. (Cited as Esdaile)

Fallon, Robert T. "John Milton and the Honorable Artillery Company." <u>Milton Quarterly</u> 9 (1975): 49-51.

Farrar, Frederic W. "The Share of America in Westminster Abbey." <u>Harper's</u> 76 (1887): 298-309.

Farrar, Reginald. <u>The Life of Frederic William Farrar</u>. London: J. Nisbet, 1904.

Fletcher, Hanslip. <u>Bombed London</u>. London: Cassell, 1947.

Fletcher, Harris F. <u>The Intellectual Development of John Milton</u>. Urbana, Ill.: Vol. I, 1956; Vol. II, 1961.

"For Favors Received." <u>Time</u> 50 (7 July 1947): 76. [On St. Mary-le-Bow]

Francis, Claude de la Roche. <u>London, Historic and Social</u>. 2 vols. Philadelphia: Coates, 1902.

French, J. Milton, ed. <u>The Life Records of John Milton</u>. 5 vols. New Brunswick: Rutgers University Press, 1949-1958.

_____. <u>Milton in Chancery</u>. New York: Modern Language Association, 1939.

_____. "Milton's Homes and Investments." <u>Philological Quarterly</u> 28 (1949) 77-97.

French, Roberts W. "A Note from Milton's Cottage." <u>Milton Newsletter</u> 3 (1969): 17-19.

_____. "St. Giles, Cripplegate." <u>Milton Newsletter</u> 2 (1968): 48-53.

Garrett, Stephen. "Barbican Developments." <u>Spectator</u>, 8 Nov. 1957, pp. 610-12.

Garrod, H. W. "Milton and Oxford." In his The Profession of Poetry. Oxford: Clarendon Press, 1929, pp. 240-53.

Garwood, H. P. "Shakespeare's Church." New Statesman and Nation, 19 Feb. 1949, p. 182.

Hampton, Charles. Ludlow Castle. Sheffield: By the author, 1977.

Hanson, Michael. 2000 Years of London. London: Country Life, 1967.

Harben, Henry A. A Dictionary of London. London: H. Jenkins, 1918.

Harland-Oxley, W. E. "The United States and St. Margaret's, Westminster." Notes and Queries, 4 July 1903, pp. 1-2; 25 July 1903, pp. 63-65; 15 Aug. 1903, pp. 123-24; 29 Aug. 1903, pp. 164-65.

Hardy, Thomas. The Hand of Ethelberta. New York: Harper, 1896.

Hare, Augustus J. C. Walks in London. 2 vols. New York: George Routledge, 1878.

Hawkes, Jacquetta. "The Poets' Fountain." New Statesman and Nation, 12 Feb. 1949, p. 150.

Hayes, John. London: A Pictorial History. London: Batsford, 1969.

_____. London from the Earliest Times to the Present Day. New York: Macmillan, 1960.

Hebb, John. Notes and Queries, 21 Nov. 1908, p. 404. [On Aldersgate Street]

Henrey, Robert. London. London: J. M. Dent, 1948.

Hibbert, Christopher. London: The Biography of a City. London: Allen Lane, 1977.

History of the Bunhill Fields Burial Ground. London: London Corporation, 1887.

Holmes, Mrs. Basil. The London Burial Grounds. New York: Macmillan, 1896.

Howson, J. S. "On the Associations of Milton with the River Dee and Cheshire." Journal of the Chester and North Wales Architectural, Archeological, and Historical Society 3 (1863-1885): 409-18.

Illustrated London News, no. 215 (17 Dec. 1949), pp. 938-39; no. 223 (26 Dec. 1953), p. 1063. [On Bunhill Fields and St. Bride's.]

Jenkinson, Wilberforce. _London Churches before the Great Fire_. London: SPCK, 1917.

Jesse, John Heneage. _London and Its Celebrities_. 3 vols. Boston: Nicolls, n.d.

Johnson, Samuel. _The Six Chief Lives_. Ed. Matthew Arnold. London: Macmillan, 1908.

Jones, Mervyn. "New Barbican." _New Statesman and Nation_, 12 Mar. 1955, p. 348.

Kent, William. _An Encyclopedia of London_. 3rd ed., New York: Macmillan, 1951; 4th ed., London: Dent, 1970.

_____. _London for the Literary Pilgrim_. London: Rockliff, 1949.

Knight, Charles, ed. _London_. 6 vols. London: Bohn, 1851.

Lang, Elsie M. _Literary London_. New York: Scribner, 1907.

Law, Dorothy Grace. _John Milton and Chalfont St. Giles_. Gerrard's Cross: By the author, 1965.

The London City Churches. 2nd ed. London: London Society, 1929.

London Times, 8 Dec. 1908, p. 10. [On the house in St. Bride's]

Masson, David. "Milton." In _In the Footsteps of the Poets_. Ed. David Masson et al. New York: Thomas Whittaker, 1894, pp. 14-104.

_____. _The Life of John Milton_. 6 vols. London: Macmillan, 1859-1880.

_____. "Local Memories of Milton." _Good Words_ 34 (1893): 39-44, 130-38, 170-75, 232-41.

Miller, Leo. "Milton's Portraits." _Milton Quarterly_, Special Issue, 1976.

A Milton Encyclopedia. Eds. William B. Hunter et al. 9 vols. Lewisburg, Pa.: Bucknell University Press, 1978-- .

A Milton Memorial. London: J. Woodley, 1862.

"The Milton Window." _Critic_ 12 (1888), 94-95.

Milton's Cottage, Chalfont St. Giles. Gerrard's Cross: Partridge and Legg, n.d.

Mitton, Geraldine E. _Buckinghamshire and Berkshire_. London: A. and C. Black, 1920.

_____. Maps of Old London. London: A. and C. Black, 1908.

_____. Where Great Men Lived in London. London: A. and C. Black, 1911.

Morgan, Dewi. Phoenix of Fleet Street: 2000 Years of St. Bride's. London: Charles Knight and Co., 1973.

Newsletter of the Friends of Milton's Cottage. June 1977 and April 1978.

Norman, G. E. M. St. Botolph's, Aldersgate. London: np., n.d.

Notes on the History of St. Giles' Church without Cripplegate. London: n.p., n.d.

Osgood, Charles G. "Milton's 'Elm Star-Proof.'" Journal of English and Germanic Philology 4 (1905), 370-78.

Page, William, ed. The Victoria History of the County of Buckingham. 4 vols. London: Constable, 1905-1927.

_____. ed. The Victoria History of the County of Oxford. Vol. I. London: Constable, 1907.

Parker, William Riley. Milton: A Biography. 2 vols. Oxford: Clarendon Press, 1968.

The Diary of Samuel Pepys. Ed. R. C. Latham and William Matthews. Vol. VII. Berkeley: University of California Press, 1972.

Pendrill, Charles. "A City Lane That Was." National Review 124 (1945): 233-41.

Pickard, Samuel Thomas. Life and Letters of John Greenleaf Whittier. 2 vols. Boston: Houghton Mifflin, 1894.

Priestley, Harold E. London: The Years of Change. London: Muller, 1966.

Rawlings, Gertrude B. The Streets of London. London: G. Bles, 1926.

Read, Allen Walker. "The Disinternment of Milton's Remains." Publications of the Modern Language Association 45 (1930): 1050-68.

Reddaway, T. F. The Rebuilding of London after the Great Fire. London: Arnold, 1940.

Rogers, Kenneth. "Bread Street: Its Ancient Signs and Houses." London Topographical Record 16 (1932): 52-76.

_____. The Mermaid and Mitre Taverns in Old London. London: Homeland Association, 1928.

_____. Old Cheapside and Poultry: Ancient Houses and Signs. London: Homeland Association, 1931.

Roscoe, Edward S. Between Thames and Chilterns. London: Faber and Gwyer, 1927.

Rossiter, Stuart. London. London: Ernest Benn, 1973.

Rowse, A. L. "The Milton Country." In his The English Past. London: Macmillan, 1951, pp. 85-112.

Rubenstein, Stanley. Historians of London. London: Owen, 1968.

Saint Giles Cripplegate. London: n.p., 1974.

Shafer, Ronald G. "In Search of Milton: A Visit to Chalfont St. Giles." Milton Quarterly 11 (1977): 50-52.

A Short History of the Church of St. Mary Aldermary. London: n.p., 1977.

Shorter, Clement. Highways and Byways in Buckinghamshire. London: Macmillan, 1910.

"A Site in Moorfields." The Living Age 233 (1902): 181-84.

Sloane, William. Notes and Queries, New Series, 6 (Oct. 1959): 357-58; 7 (June 1960): 220-22. [On Milton at Cambridge]

Smith, Al. Dictionary of the City of London. Newton Abbot: David & Charles, 1970.

Smyth, Charles. Church and Parish. London: SPCK, 1955.

_____. "The Commons' Church." Spectator, 3 March 1950, p. 268.

Stow, John. Survey of London. Ed. Robert Seymour. 2 vols. London: T. Read, 1733-1755.

_____. Survey of London. Ed. Charles C. Kingsford. 2 vols. Oxford: Clarendon Press, 1908. (Cited as Stow)

The Survey of London. London: The London County Council and The Greater London Council, 1900-- .
    Vol. 3 (1912). The Parish of St. Giles in the Fields.
      5 (1914). The Parish of St. Giles in the Fields.
      6 (1915). The Parish of Hammersmith.

Vol. 10 (1926). The Parish of St. Margaret,
               Westminster.
   13 (1930). The Parish of St. Margaret,
               Westminster.
   14 (1931). The Parish of St. Margaret,
               Westminster.
   16 (1935). The Parish of St. Martin's in
               the Fields.
   25 (1955). The Parish of St. George's in
               the Fields.

"Table Talk." Gentleman's Magazine 264 (1888): 623-24.

Taylor, Gordon. Saint Giles-in-the-Fields: Its Part in
    History. London: n.p., 1977.

Thornbury, George Walter. Old and New London. Rev.
    ed. 6 vols. London: Cassell, 1887-1893.

Tillyard, E. M. W. "Arnold on Milton." In his Studies
    in Milton. London: Chatto & Windus, 1955,
    pp. 1-7.

Todd, Rev. H. J. Some Account of the Life and Writings
    of John Milton. London: R. Gilbert, 1826.

Trent, Christopher. Greater London: Its Growth and
    Development through Two Thousand Years.
    London: Phoenix House, 1965.

Venables, Edmund. Notes and Queries, 8 Dec. 1888,
    p. 454 [On All Hallows]

Webb, Edward A. The Records of St. Bartholomew's
    Priory and of the Church and Parish of St. Bar-
    tholomew the Great, West Smithfield. 2 vols.
    Oxford: Oxford University Press, 1921.

Westlake, Herbert F. St. Margaret's, Westminster.
    London: Smith, Elder and Co., 1914.

Wheatley, Henry B. London Past and Present. 3 vols.
    London: J. Murray, 1891.

_____. "Milton and London." Academy, 27 Aug. 1898,
    201-202.

Whitaker's Almanack. 107th ed. London: J. Whitaker,
    1975.

Whitaker-Wilson, Cecil. Whitehall Palace. London:
    Frederick Muller, 1934.

Whitting, Philip D. A History of Hammersmith. London:
    Hammersmith Local History Group, 1965.

The Winston Churchill Memorial and Library. Fulton,
    Missouri: Westminster College, n.d.

Wolfe, Don M. Milton and His England. Princeton: Princeton University Press, 1971.

Youngblood, Ed. "To Milton by Motorcycle: An Unlikely Progress." Milton Quarterly 11 (1977): 52-54.

139